SCOTLAND UNVEILED :A TRAVEL PREPARATION GUIDE

TOMAS GRAY

TABLE OF CONTENTS

CHAPTER 1. Introduction to Scotland

1.1 Overview of Scotland's Regions

Overview of Scotland:

Scotland is a country located in the northern part of the United Kingdom (UK). It shares its southern border with England and is surrounded by the Atlantic Ocean to the west and north, the North Sea to the northeast, and the Irish Sea to the south. Scotland has a rich history, unique culture, and stunning natural landscapes that draw visitors from around the world.

Geography and Landscapes:

Scotland's geography is diverse and characterized by rugged coastlines, rolling hills, and expansive moorlands. The country is known for its mountainous terrain, with the Scottish Highlands being the most prominent mountain range. Ben Nevis, located in the Highlands, is the highest peak in the UK. The Lowlands, in contrast, are more flat and fertile, with major cities like Glasgow and Edinburgh situated in this region.

Culture and Heritage:

Scotland has a distinct cultural identity that manifests through its music, dance, literature, and festivals. The traditional Scottish music is often accompanied by bagpipes, and the country is famous for its Highland Games, which showcase traditional sports like caber tossing and hammer throwing. Scottish literature has also made significant contributions to the world, with renowned authors like Sir Walter Scott and Robert Burns.

The Scots have a strong sense of national pride, and their rich heritage is evident in the preservation of historic sites such as Edinburgh Castle, Stirling Castle, and the prehistoric village of Skara Brae in the Orkney Islands.

Economy:

Scotland's economy is diverse and encompasses various industries, including oil and gas, renewable energy, tourism, agriculture, and whisky production. The discovery of North Sea oil in the 1970s significantly boosted Scotland's economy, leading to the establishment of major oil and gas companies in Aberdeen, known as the "Oil Capital of Europe."

Tourism plays a vital role in the Scottish economy, with visitors attracted to the country's castles, picturesque landscapes, and vibrant cities. Scotland's whisky industry is world-renowned, producing famous brands like Scotch whisky.

Politics:

Scotland has its own devolved government, known as the Scottish Parliament, located in Edinburgh. The parliament has powers over areas such as education, health, and transport, while defense, foreign affairs, and immigration remain under the control of the UK Parliament in Westminster, London.

Over the years, there have been discussions and debates about Scotland's constitutional status within the UK. The Scottish independence referendum in 2014 saw the majority of Scots voting to remain in the UK. However, the issue of independence has remained a prominent political topic, with ongoing discussions about the possibility of another referendum in the future.

Scotland's Regions:

Scotland is divided into several distinct regions, each with its own unique characteristics and attractions:

1. Central Belt: This region encompasses the major cities of Glasgow and Edinburgh, along with other towns and cities. It is the economic heart of Scotland and is known for its cultural offerings, historical sites, and vibrant nightlife.

2. Scottish Highlands: The Highlands are renowned for their breathtaking landscapes, including rugged mountains, serene lochs, and ancient castles. It is a popular destination for outdoor enthusiasts and nature lovers.

3. Scottish Lowlands: The Lowlands are characterized by more gentle landscapes, fertile farmlands, and charming villages. This region is home to historic sites, picturesque countryside, and the famous Loch Ness.

4. Scottish Islands: Scotland has a multitude of islands, each with its own character and charm. The Orkney and Shetland Islands, in the far north, offer fascinating ancient history and unique wildlife. The Isle of Skye, in the Inner Hebrides, is known for its dramatic landscapes.

5. Southern Scotland: This region includes the Scottish Borders and Dumfries and Galloway. It is known for its historical connections, with numerous castles and abbeys, as well as its scenic beauty.

6. Northeast Scotland: This area includes the city of Aberdeen and is known for its oil and gas industry, as well as its stunning coastline and charming fishing villages.

Each region contributes to the overall diversity and appeal of Scotland, making it a captivating and multifaceted destination for travelers and locals alike.

1.2 Climate and Best Time to Visit

Scotland's climate is notoriously changeable, influenced by its geographical location and proximity to the Atlantic Ocean. Despite its reputation for unpredictable weather, Scotland offers a unique and captivating experience for visitors throughout the year. This guide will explore Scotland's climate, weather patterns, and the best times to visit, ensuring you make the most of your trip to this beautiful and diverse country.

Climate Overview:

Scotland's climate is classified as temperate maritime, characterized by mild winters and cool summers. The Atlantic Ocean plays a significant role in shaping the weather, moderating extreme temperature fluctuations. The Gulf Stream, a warm ocean current, also influences the climate, making it milder than expected for its northern latitude.

Seasonal Weather Patterns:

1. Spring (March to May): Spring in Scotland is a delightful time to visit as the country comes alive with colorful blooms and blossoms. Average temperatures range from 8°C to 12°C (46°F to 54°F). However, be prepared for some rain as showers are common throughout the season.

2. Summer (June to August): Summer is the peak tourist season in Scotland, and it is no surprise given the relatively mild temperatures ranging from 12°C to 19°C (54°F to 66°F). Days are long, with the sun setting late in the evening, providing ample time to explore. However, expect occasional rain showers and pack some warmer layers as temperatures can vary.

3. Autumn (September to November): Autumn paints Scotland in stunning hues of red and gold as the foliage changes. Temperatures cool down, ranging from 7°C to 13°C (45°F to 55°F). It is a great time for outdoor activities, and the countryside offers a picturesque setting for long walks and hikes.

4. Winter (December to February): Winter can be cold in Scotland, with average temperatures ranging from 2°C to 6°C (36°F to 43°F). In the Highlands, you might encounter snow, creating a magical winter wonderland. It's an ideal time for winter sports enthusiasts and those seeking a cozy escape in front of a roaring fire.

Best Time to Visit:

The best time to visit Scotland depends on your preferences and interests. Here are some considerations for each season:

1. Summer (June to August): Summer is the most popular time to visit Scotland, particularly for tourists seeking pleasant weather, longer daylight hours, and a vibrant atmosphere. However, keep in mind that popular tourist destinations can get

crowded during this period, and accommodation prices may be higher.

2. Spring (March to May) and Autumn (September to November): These shoulder seasons offer a fantastic balance between milder weather, fewer crowds, and a beautiful backdrop of blooming flowers in spring or colorful foliage in autumn. It's an excellent time for exploring the outdoors without the peak-season hustle.

3. Winter (December to February): If you enjoy winter sports, picturesque snow-capped landscapes, and cozy evenings by the fireplace, visiting Scotland during the winter months can be a magical experience. Just be prepared for colder temperatures and the possibility of travel disruptions due to snow.

Festivals and Events:

Scotland hosts a variety of festivals and events throughout the year, adding cultural and traditional charm to your visit. Here are some noteworthy events to consider when planning your trip:

1. Edinburgh International Festival (August): This renowned arts festival showcases world-class

performances in music, theater, opera, and dance, attracting artists and spectators from around the globe.

2. Edinburgh Festival Fringe (August): Held alongside the International Festival, the Fringe is the world's largest arts festival, featuring thousands of performances ranging from comedy to drama, and everything in between.

3. Royal Edinburgh Military Tattoo (August): Witness an unforgettable display of military bands, dancers, and performers against the backdrop of Edinburgh Castle.

4. Hogmanay (New Year's Eve): Scotland's famous New Year's Eve celebration takes place with festivities, concerts, and the spectacular Edinburgh Hogmanay Street Party.

Practical Tips for Visiting Scotland:

1. Pack for All Weather: Scotland's weather can change rapidly, so be prepared for rain, wind, and sun. Layered clothing and a waterproof jacket are essential items to include in your packing list.

2. Transportation: Scotland offers an extensive network of trains, buses, and ferries, making it easy to travel between cities and explore the countryside. Consider purchasing a travel pass or a Scottish Heritage Pass to access various attractions.

3. Reservations: During peak tourist seasons, it's advisable to book accommodations and tours in advance to secure your preferred options.

4. Respect the Environment: Scotland's stunning landscapes are a precious resource. Follow the "Leave No Trace" principles and respect wildlife and local communities during your visit.

Scotland's climate offers a unique experience in each season, from vibrant summers with long daylight hours to picturesque autumns and snowy winters. The best time to visit depends on your preferences and interests. Whether you're interested in exploring the historic cities, hiking in the majestic Highlands, or immersing yourself in cultural festivals, Scotland has something to offer year-round. Plan your trip wisely, and you'll undoubtedly fall in love with the beauty, charm, and warmth of Scotland and its people.

1.3 Cultural Etiquette and Tips

When traveling to Scotland, it's essential to familiarize yourself with the local cultural etiquette and customs to ensure a respectful and enjoyable experience. Scotland boasts a rich heritage and unique traditions that shape the daily lives of its people. Understanding and embracing these customs will help you connect with the locals and appreciate the country's vibrant culture. Here are some key cultural etiquette and tips to keep in mind during your visit to Scotland.

1. Greetings and Politeness:

- Handshakes: When meeting someone for the first time, a firm handshake is a common greeting. Maintain eye contact and smile to convey sincerity and respect.

- Polite Phrases: Using polite phrases like "please" and "thank you" is essential in Scottish culture. Expressing gratitude and acknowledging others' efforts is highly valued.

2. Punctuality:

Being punctual is considered a sign of respect in Scottish culture. Arrive on time for appointments, meetings, and social gatherings. If you anticipate being late, it's courteous to inform the other party in advance.

3. Personal Space:

Scots generally appreciate personal space, so avoid standing too close to someone while engaging in conversation. Maintaining a comfortable distance shows respect for their personal boundaries.

4. Table Manners:

When dining in Scotland, adhere to traditional table manners:

- Toasting: When someone proposes a toast, it is customary to raise your glass and clink glasses with those around you before taking a sip.

- Cutlery: Start using cutlery from the outside and work your way in with each course. When finished, place your knife and fork together on the plate.

- Tipping: Tipping is not obligatory, but leaving a small gratuity for good service is appreciated. In restaurants, a 10-15% tip is common, but feel free to adjust according to the level of service.

5. Dress Code:

Scotland has a relatively casual dress code for most occasions. In urban areas, smart-casual attire is generally acceptable in restaurants and social events. However, some places, such as high-end restaurants or cultural events, may have more formal dress requirements. Check in advance if unsure.

6. Scottish Language and Pronunciation:

Although English is the official language, Scotland has its own unique dialects and regional accents. While most Scots speak standard English, you may encounter some local terms and expressions. Don't be afraid to ask for clarification if you don't understand something, as Scots are generally friendly and happy to help.

7. Participating in Traditions:

Scotland is rich in traditions and cultural events. If you have the opportunity to participate, embrace the experience with enthusiasm. For example:

- Ceilidh Dancing: Ceilidh dances are a traditional form of social dancing in Scotland. Don't be shy to join in the fun and learn the steps.

- Hogmanay: Scotland's famous New Year's Eve celebration, Hogmanay, involves various customs such as "first-footing." If you're invited into someone's home during this time, bringing a small gift or token of goodwill is customary.

- Tartan and Kilts: Traditional Scottish attire, including kilts and tartan patterns, is commonly worn during special events and festivals. Show respect for the tradition by not making fun of or mocking such clothing.

8. Photography and Privacy:

When taking photographs, especially in more rural or less touristy areas, it's considerate to ask for permission before photographing locals or their property. Respect people's privacy and avoid photographing individuals without their consent.

9. Religion and Customs:

Scotland has a diverse religious landscape, with Christianity being the dominant religion. Respect places of worship and adhere to any guidelines or dress codes if visiting religious sites. Be aware of local customs and traditions, especially during important religious holidays or events.

10. Being Open and Friendly:

Scots are known for their warmth and friendliness. Be open to engaging in conversations with locals, and don't hesitate to ask for recommendations or advice. Showing genuine interest in Scotland's culture and history will often lead to meaningful interactions and connections.

By embracing Scotland's cultural etiquette and customs, you will not only demonstrate respect for the country's heritage but also enhance your travel experience. Engaging with locals, participating in traditions, and appreciating the nuances of Scottish life will create lasting memories and leave you with a deeper understanding of this fascinating and welcoming country. Remember to approach your interactions with an open mind, a friendly demeanor, and a willingness to embrace the beauty of Scotland's culture.

CHAPTER 2. Planning Your Trip to Scotland

2.1 Visa and Travel Documents

Before embarking on your journey to the enchanting landscapes of Scotland, it's crucial to understand the visa and travel document requirements that apply to your nationality. The United Kingdom, of which Scotland is a part, has specific regulations governing entry and stay for tourists. Ensuring that you have the right paperwork will make your trip hassle-free and memorable.

Visa Requirements

Whether you need a visa to visit Scotland depends on your nationality. The UK operates a points-based immigration system, and different rules apply to citizens of European Union (EU) and European Economic Area (EEA) countries compared to citizens of non-EEA countries.

EU and EEA Citizens

Until the end of 2020, citizens of EU and EEA countries enjoyed the freedom of movement within the UK, including Scotland, due to the UK's membership in the EU. However, with the conclusion of the Brexit transition period, new rules came into effect.

If you are an EU or EEA citizen who was living in the UK by December 31, 2020, you may be eligible to apply for the EU Settlement Scheme, which grants you the right to continue living and working in the UK, including Scotland. This scheme allows you to secure either "settled status" or "pre-settled status," depending on the duration of your residence.

For EU and EEA citizens who wish to visit Scotland for short stays (up to six months), a visa is not required. You can enter with a valid passport. However, it's recommended to carry documentation that proves the purpose of your visit, such as hotel reservations, return flight tickets, and evidence of sufficient funds.

Non-EEA Citizens

If you are a citizen of a non-EEA country, you will likely need a visa to visit Scotland. The type of visa you require will depend on the purpose of your visit. The UK offers various visa categories, including tourist visas, business visas, study visas, and more. It's essential to apply for the correct visa before you travel.

Tourist visas typically allow you to stay in the UK, including Scotland, for up to six months. To apply for a tourist visa, you'll need to provide evidence of your intended stay, ties to your home country, financial capability to support yourself during your visit, and other relevant documents.

Required Travel Documents

While a visa is a primary requirement for entry, other travel documents are equally important to ensure a smooth journey to Scotland.

Passport

All travelers, regardless of their nationality, must have a valid passport to enter Scotland. Your passport should be valid for the duration of your stay, and it's recommended to have a few months' validity beyond your planned departure date.

Entry Clearance

If you are a non-EEA citizen who requires a visa, you'll need to obtain entry clearance before traveling to the UK. Entry clearance is a document stamped in your passport that confirms your eligibility to enter the country.

Return Tickets

Immigration officials may ask for proof of onward travel, so it's advisable to carry return flight tickets or evidence of your plans to leave the UK at the end of your visit.

Accommodation and Itinerary

Having hotel reservations or an itinerary that outlines your travel plans can help demonstrate the purpose of your visit and your intention to abide by the terms of your visa.

Immigration Control and Arrival

Upon arriving in Scotland, you'll go through immigration control at your port of entry. This is where immigration officials will review your travel documents, including your visa if applicable, and ask about the purpose of your visit. It's essential to answer their questions truthfully and provide any requested documents to avoid any complications.

Extending Your Stay

If you're in Scotland and wish to extend your stay beyond the duration of your visa, you must apply for an extension before your current visa expires. Extensions are subject to eligibility criteria and the purpose of your visit.

Visiting Scotland can be a dream come true, but ensuring you have the correct visa and travel documents is essential for a hassle-free experience. EU and EEA citizens now need to consider the EU Settlement Scheme, while non-EEA citizens should research the appropriate visa category and apply in advance. Remember that regulations and requirements can change, so it's wise to check with the official UK government websites or consult the nearest UK embassy or consulate before your journey.

2.2 Choosing the Right Itinerary

Planning the right itinerary is crucial for making the most of your trip to Scotland. Here's an extensive guide on how to choose the perfect itinerary:

Choosing the Right Itinerary for Your Trip to Scotland

Scotland's breathtaking landscapes, rich history, and vibrant culture offer a plethora of experiences for travelers. Crafting the right itinerary is essential to ensure you capture the essence of this enchanting country. Whether you're interested in history, nature, or urban exploration, here's a comprehensive guide to help you plan your ideal trip.

Determine the Duration of Your Trip

The first step in crafting the perfect itinerary is deciding how long you'll be in Scotland. The country offers a diverse range of experiences, so the duration of your stay will impact how much you can explore. A week is a good starting point to cover major highlights, but if you have more time, you can delve deeper into specific regions.

Identify Your Interests

Scotland boasts a variety of attractions, each catering to different interests. Are you a history enthusiast, a nature lover, a whisky connoisseur, or someone who appreciates vibrant city life? Identifying your interests will help you prioritize what to include in your itinerary.

Historical Exploration

If history intrigues you, Edinburgh and Stirling are must-visit cities. Explore the historic Edinburgh Castle, walk along the Royal Mile, and visit the Stirling Castle. Consider venturing to the prehistoric village of Skara Brae in Orkney or the medieval stronghold of Eilean Donan Castle.

Natural Wonders

Scotland's natural beauty is undeniable. The Scottish Highlands offer breathtaking landscapes, including Glencoe, Loch Ness, and the Isle of Skye. Hike in Cairngorms National Park or marvel at the dramatic coastline in the North Coast 500 route.

Urban Adventures

For urban experiences, Edinburgh and Glasgow are vibrant cities with distinct characters. Discover Edinburgh's cultural festivals, the Edinburgh Fringe being a highlight, or explore Glasgow's art scene, including the Kelvingrove Art Gallery and the Riverside Museum.

Whisky and Culinary Delights

Whisky aficionados will relish a visit to distilleries in regions like Speyside and Islay. Delve into Scottish cuisine by trying haggis, neeps and tatties, and fresh seafood.

Plan a Balanced Itinerary

Striking a balance between different activities is key to a fulfilling trip. Mix historical sightseeing with outdoor adventures, and urban exploration with serene countryside escapes. Avoid cramming too much into a single day to ensure you have time to absorb each experience fully.

Consider Travel Distances

Scotland's landscapes are stunning, but they can require considerable travel time between destinations. Be mindful of the distances between attractions and plan your itinerary to minimize long stretches of driving. Consider basing yourself in central locations to cut down on travel time.

Embrace Local Experiences

Interacting with locals can add depth to your journey. Attend traditional ceilidh dances, visit local pubs, and engage in conversations with residents. Their insights can lead you to hidden gems and provide a more authentic experience.

Be Flexible

While planning is essential, leave room for flexibility. Weather can be unpredictable, and unexpected opportunities may arise. Having a loose structure allows you to adapt to changing circumstances.

Seek Professional Advice

If crafting an itinerary seems overwhelming, consider consulting travel agencies or experts specializing in Scotland. They can offer insights into lesser-known attractions, suggest efficient routes, and ensure you're not missing out on any must-see sites.

Crafting the perfect itinerary for your trip to Scotland involves a combination of thorough research, self-awareness of your interests, and an openness to the unexpected. Scotland's diverse offerings mean you can create a personalized journey that reflects your passions and allows you to savor every moment in this captivating country.

Example of a good itinerary
Here's a 7-day itinerary:

Day 1: Arrival in Edinburgh
- Arrive in Edinburgh, check into your accommodation.
- Explore the historic Edinburgh Castle.
- Stroll down the Royal Mile and explore the Old Town.

Day 2: Edinburgh
- Visit the Palace of Holyroodhouse.
- Walk up Arthur's Seat for panoramic views of the city.
- Explore the National Museum of Scotland.

Day 3: Stirling and Loch Lomond
- Drive to Stirling and visit Stirling Castle.
- Head to Loch Lomond for a scenic boat ride or hike.
- Overnight stay near Loch Lomond.

Day 4: Glencoe and Fort William
- Drive through the stunning Glencoe Valley.
- Continue to Fort William and explore the town.
- Consider taking the Jacobite Steam Train if interested.

Day 5: Isle of Skye
- Drive to the Isle of Skye.
- Visit the Fairy Pools, Old Man of Storr, and Portree.
- Enjoy the rugged landscapes and dramatic cliffs.

Day 6: Inverness and Loch Ness
- Drive to Inverness, the capital of the Highlands.
- Explore the city and visit Inverness Castle.
- Take a cruise or walk along Loch Ness.

Day 7: Cairngorms National Park
- Drive to Cairngorms National Park.
- Enjoy outdoor activities like hiking, cycling, or wildlife spotting.
- Depart from Inverness or extend your stay.

2.3 Budgeting and Cost Considerations

Budgeting and cost considerations are crucial when planning a trip to Scotland or anywhere. Here's an extensive guide to help you manage your expenses and make the most of your journey:

1. Transportation:
- Flights: Search for deals on flights to major cities like Edinburgh or Glasgow. Booking in advance and being flexible with travel dates can save you money.

- Rental Cars: If you plan to explore rural areas, renting a car might be beneficial. Compare prices from different rental companies and book in advance for better rates.
- Public Transport: Scotland has an efficient public transport system, including trains and buses. Consider getting a rail pass for unlimited train travel within a certain period.

2. Accommodation:
- Hotels: Look for budget-friendly hotels, hostels, or guesthouses. Booking platforms often offer discounts for early reservations.
- Airbnb: Renting a private room or apartment through Airbnb can be cost-effective, especially for groups.
- Hostels: Scotland has numerous hostels that provide affordable accommodations with shared facilities.

3. Food and Dining:
- Eating Out: Opt for local eateries and pubs rather than touristy restaurants. Many places offer lunchtime deals or pre-theater menus at discounted prices.
- Grocery Stores: Consider buying snacks and easy-to-make meals from grocery stores to save on dining costs.

- Self-Catering: If your accommodation has a kitchen, prepare some of your meals to cut down expenses.

4. Attractions and Activities:
- Historic Scotland Pass: If you plan to visit multiple historic sites and castles, consider purchasing a Historic Scotland Explorer Pass for savings.
- Free Attractions: Scotland offers plenty of free attractions, including stunning natural landscapes, city walks, and some museums.
- Tours: Research and compare tour prices for activities like whisky tasting, city tours, or boat trips. Booking online might offer better deals.

5. Travel Insurance:
- Don't skimp on travel insurance. It's essential to have coverage for medical emergencies, trip cancellations, and unexpected incidents.

6. Currency and Payment:
- Currency Exchange: Check exchange rates and consider exchanging currency before your trip for better rates.
- Credit Cards: Notify your bank about your travel plans and consider using credit cards with no foreign transaction fees.

7. Budgeting Tips:
- Create a detailed itinerary with estimated costs for accommodation, transportation, meals, and activities.
- Set a daily spending limit and track your expenses using apps or notebooks.
- Allocate a buffer for unexpected expenses or splurges.
- Research local deals, discounts, and coupons.

8. Seasonal Considerations:
- Peak vs. Off-Peak: Traveling during the off-peak season (usually autumn and spring) can result in lower prices for accommodations and attractions.
- Festivals and Events: Be aware of major festivals or events that might drive up accommodation prices.

9. Souvenirs and Shopping:
- Allocate a specific budget for souvenirs and stick to it.
- Look for local markets or craft fairs where you might find unique items at reasonable prices.

Remember that costs can vary widely based on your preferences and travel style. By planning ahead, researching discounts, and making informed choices, you can enjoy a memorable trip to Scotland without breaking the bank.

2.4 Accommodation Options

Finding the right accommodation is a key aspect of planning your trip to Scotland. Here's an in-depth guide to various accommodation options you can consider:

1. Hotels:
- Scotland offers a range of hotels from budget to luxury. You'll find international chains as well as charming boutique hotels.
- Consider location when choosing a hotel, as being centrally located can save you transportation costs and time.
- Booking websites often provide deals, so compare prices and read reviews before making a choice.

2. Bed and Breakfasts (B&Bs):
- B&Bs provide a cozy and personalized experience. They are often run by locals and offer hearty breakfasts.
- Ideal for travelers seeking a more intimate atmosphere and a chance to interact with hosts and other guests.

3. Hostels:

- Scotland has a variety of hostels catering to budget-conscious travelers.
- Hostels offer dormitory-style rooms with shared facilities. Some also have private rooms.
- Perfect for solo travelers, backpackers, or those looking to socialize and meet fellow travelers.

4. Guesthouses and Inns:
- Guesthouses and inns are similar to B&Bs but may have more rooms and facilities.
- They provide a comfortable and homey atmosphere, often with traditional Scottish decor.

5. Self-Catering Apartments and Cottages:
- If you prefer independence and privacy, consider renting a self-catering apartment or cottage.
- These options come with kitchens, allowing you to cook your meals and save on dining costs.

6. Airbnb and Vacation Rentals:
- Airbnb offers a wide range of accommodations, from private rooms to entire apartments or houses.
- You can find unique stays in local neighborhoods, giving you a more authentic experience.

7. Castle Stays:
- For a truly unique experience, you can stay in a Scottish castle.

- Some castles have been converted into luxury accommodations, offering historical charm and modern amenities.

8. Farm Stays:
- If you're interested in rural life, consider a farm stay. You can experience the countryside, interact with animals, and enjoy fresh produce.

9. Glamping and Camping:
- Scotland's stunning natural landscapes make it an ideal destination for glamping (luxury camping).
- Many campsites offer facilities like showers and kitchens, making camping a comfortable option.

10. Luxury Resorts:
- Scotland boasts luxury resorts with world-class amenities, spa facilities, and breathtaking views.
- Popular for special occasions or those seeking a pampered getaway.

11. Unusual Accommodations:
- Scotland offers unique options like lighthouses, treehouses, and even whisky barrels converted into accommodation.
- These options provide a memorable stay and a story to tell.

Considerations:
- Location: Choose accommodations near your planned activities to minimize travel time and costs.
- Budget: Set a budget and explore options that fit within it.
- Group Size: Accommodations can vary based on the number of travelers. Some places are ideal for couples, while others are more suitable for families or groups.
- Amenities: Consider your preferences for amenities like Wi-Fi, parking, and breakfast.

Remember to book accommodations well in advance, especially during peak tourist seasons. Scotland's diverse range of accommodations ensures there's something for every traveler, whether you're seeking luxury, authenticity, or budget-friendly options.

CHAPTER 3. Must-Visit Destinations in Scotland

3.1 Edinburgh: Historic Capital City

Edinburgh, the historic capital city of Scotland, is a captivating blend of rich history, stunning architecture, and vibrant culture.

1. Edinburgh Castle:
- Dominating the city's skyline, this iconic castle offers panoramic views and a glimpse into Scotland's royal history.
- Explore the Crown Jewels, the Stone of Destiny, and the military history of the castle.

2. The Royal Mile:
- A historic thoroughfare that runs through the heart of the Old Town, lined with shops, pubs, and historic sites.
- Don't miss attractions like St. Giles' Cathedral, the Real Mary King's Close, and the Museum of Edinburgh.

3. Holyrood Palace and Park:
- The official residence of the British monarch in Scotland, offering guided tours of the lavish State Apartments and beautiful gardens.

- Adjacent to the palace, explore the picturesque Holyrood Park and hike up Arthur's Seat for breathtaking city views.

4. National Museum of Scotland:
- Discover Scotland's diverse history, culture, and natural world in this fascinating museum.
- The museum features interactive exhibits, ancient artifacts, and displays on science and innovation.

5. Princes Street and Gardens:
- A bustling shopping street with a mix of high-street and designer stores, boasting stunning views of the Edinburgh Castle.
- Adjacent to the street, enjoy the serene Princes Street Gardens for a leisurely stroll.

6. Calton Hill:
- Offers panoramic views of the city, along with iconic landmarks like the National Monument and the Nelson Monument.
- A popular spot to watch the sunrise or sunset.

7. Edinburgh Festival Fringe:
- If visiting in August, immerse yourself in the world's largest arts festival, featuring thousands of performances across various genres.

8. Scottish Parliament Building:
- A modern architectural marvel, offering guided tours to learn about Scotland's devolved government.

9. Old Town and New Town:
- Wander through the atmospheric medieval streets of the Old Town, contrasted by the elegant Georgian New Town.
- Both areas are UNESCO World Heritage Sites and offer a blend of history and modernity.

10. Scotch Whisky Experience:
- Learn about Scotland's national drink through interactive exhibits and whisky tasting sessions.

11. Dynamic Earth:
- An educational attraction that explores Earth's history, geology, and natural forces through interactive displays.

12. Culinary Delights:
- Sample traditional Scottish dishes like haggis, neeps and tatties, and enjoy whisky tasting experiences.
- Edinburgh's dining scene offers a variety of international cuisines as well.

13. Festivals and Events:

- Aside from the Edinburgh Festival Fringe, the city hosts a variety of events throughout the year, including the Edinburgh International Festival, Hogmanay (New Year's Eve) celebrations, and more.

14. Ghost Tours:

- Explore the city's spooky side with guided ghost tours through its haunted closes and underground vaults.

15. Local Markets:

- Visit the Grassmarket area for unique shops, boutiques, and vibrant markets.

Edinburgh's rich history, captivating landmarks, and vibrant cultural scene make it a must-visit destination for travelers. Whether you're interested in history, art, architecture, or simply soaking up the atmosphere of this enchanting city, Edinburgh has something to offer for everyone.

3.2 Glasgow: Vibrant Arts and Culture Hub

Glasgow is a dynamic and culturally rich city in Scotland known for its vibrant arts and cultural scene.

1. Kelvingrove Art Gallery and Museum:
- A must-visit attraction housing an impressive collection of artworks, historical artifacts, and natural history exhibits.
- Explore everything from Renaissance masterpieces to ancient Egyptian mummies.

2. The Lighthouse:
- Scotland's Centre for Design and Architecture, this unique building offers exhibitions, galleries, and a viewing platform with panoramic views of the city.

3. Glasgow School of Art:
- Designed by Charles Rennie Mackintosh, this iconic building is a masterpiece of Art Nouveau architecture.
- Take guided tours to learn about its history and impact on design.

4. Riverside Museum:
- A fascinating transport museum showcasing Glasgow's history through an eclectic collection of vintage cars, bicycles, and even a recreated street from the past.

5. Gallery of Modern Art (GoMA):

- Home to a diverse collection of contemporary artworks, installations, and exhibitions by both local and international artists.

6. Street Art Scene:
- Explore Glasgow's ever-evolving street art scene, with murals and graffiti decorating buildings and walls throughout the city.

7. Merchant City:
- This trendy district is known for its art galleries, independent boutiques, and vibrant nightlife.
- The annual Merchant City Festival celebrates the area's arts and culture with performances and events.

8. Trongate 103:
- A creative hub housing galleries, artist studios, and creative spaces, offering a peek into Glasgow's thriving artistic community.

9. Theatre and Performing Arts:
- Glasgow boasts a variety of theaters, including the Citizens Theatre and the Tron Theatre, offering a range of performances from drama to comedy.

10. Music Scene:

- Known for its music heritage, Glasgow has a vibrant live music scene. Don't miss King Tut's Wah Wah Hut, a renowned music venue.

11. Glasgow Film Theatre:
- A historic cinema showcasing a mix of mainstream, independent, and foreign films, along with special events and film festivals.

12. West End:
- A charming area filled with quaint cafes, boutiques, and art galleries. It's also home to the University of Glasgow and its stunning architecture.

13. Hidden Lane Studios:
- A hidden gem featuring artist studios, craft shops, and galleries in a picturesque lane in the West End.

14. Edinburgh Festival Fringe:
- If visiting during August, you can enjoy an array of arts and cultural performances as part of the Edinburgh Festival Fringe.

15. Cuisine and Nightlife:
- Glasgow's culinary scene offers a mix of international flavors, and its nightlife is known for its diverse selection of bars, pubs, and live music venues.

16. Festivals and Events:
- The city hosts a variety of events, including the Celtic Connections music festival and the Glasgow International Festival of Visual Art.

Glasgow's thriving arts and culture scene, along with its friendly atmosphere, makes it a destination that's both inspiring and welcoming. From world-class museums to hidden art studios, there's something for every art and culture enthusiast to discover in this vibrant Scottish city.

3.3 The Highlands: Majestic Landscapes and Castles

Highlands:
Welcome to the captivating world of the Scottish Highlands, a region renowned for its rugged landscapes, mystical allure, and historic castles. This travel guide will take you on an immersive journey through the majestic landscapes and enchanting castles that make the Highlands a must-visit destination for travelers seeking both natural beauty and cultural richness.

Majestic Landscapes:
The Scottish Highlands boast some of the most breathtaking landscapes on Earth. From rolling

hills and serene lochs to dramatic mountains and lush glens, the natural beauty of this region is unparalleled. The iconic Ben Nevis, the UK's highest peak, offers hikers and mountaineers an exhilarating challenge, while the tranquil beauty of Loch Ness has captured the imagination of generations with its deep, mysterious waters.

The Highlands are a paradise for outdoor enthusiasts, offering a wide range of activities including hiking, fishing, cycling, and wildlife watching. The Cairngorms National Park, with its diverse ecosystems and rare species, is a treasure trove for nature lovers. The hauntingly beautiful Glen Coe, with its steep-sided valleys and rugged terrain, is a favorite among photographers and adventurers alike.

Enchanting Castles:
The Scottish Highlands are home to some of the world's most captivating castles, each steeped in history and folklore. Eilean Donan Castle, perched on an island at the confluence of three lochs, is a symbol of Scotland's medieval past. Urquhart Castle, overlooking the enigmatic Loch Ness, offers visitors a glimpse into its turbulent history and stunning views of the surrounding landscape.

Cawdor Castle, famous for its association with Shakespeare's "Macbeth," is a blend of medieval and modern architecture, surrounded by picturesque gardens. Blair Castle, nestled within the Cairngorms, showcases opulent interiors and extensive grounds, providing insight into the lives of Scottish nobility.

Cultural Richness:
The Highlands are deeply rooted in Scottish culture and tradition. Traditional Highland games, featuring events like caber tossing and hammer throwing, offer a glimpse into the region's heritage. The haunting sound of bagpipes resonates through the glens, and you can experience the rich traditions of ceilidh dancing and tartan weaving.

Local Cuisine:
No visit to the Highlands is complete without savoring its culinary delights. Indulge in hearty dishes like haggis, neeps and tatties, and smoked salmon, all prepared using fresh, local ingredients. Pair your meal with a dram of fine Scotch whisky, distilled in the region for centuries.

Planning Your Trip:
When planning your Highland adventure, consider the best time to visit. Summer offers longer days

and milder weather, ideal for outdoor activities, while autumn paints the landscapes with hues of gold and red. Accommodation options range from cozy bed and breakfasts to luxury lodges, often surrounded by stunning vistas.

The Scottish Highlands are a destination that captures the heart and soul of every traveler. Majestic landscapes, enchanting castles, rich culture, and warm hospitality come together to create an experience that lingers in your memory long after you've left. Whether you're an outdoor enthusiast, a history buff, or simply someone seeking beauty and tranquility, the Highlands will undoubtedly leave an indelible mark on your travel journey.

3.4 Isle of Skye: Natural Beauty and Outdoor Adventures

Welcome to the enchanting Isle of Skye, a jewel nestled off the west coast of Scotland. Known for its breathtaking landscapes, rugged coastline, and outdoor adventures, Skye offers a unique blend of natural beauty and exhilarating experiences. This travel guide will take you on a journey through the island's stunning landscapes, outdoor activities, and cultural treasures.

Natural Beauty:
The Isle of Skye is a paradise for nature enthusiasts. From the moment you set foot on the island, you'll be greeted by stunning vistas that include dramatic cliffs, serene lochs, and lush glens. The iconic Old Man of Storr, a majestic pinnacle of rock, is a magnet for hikers and photographers, offering panoramic views of the island's stunning landscape.

The Quiraing, a geological marvel, features otherworldly rock formations and winding paths that lead you through an awe-inspiring terrain. Fairy Pools, a series of crystal-clear pools and waterfalls, present the perfect opportunity for a refreshing dip or a leisurely stroll along the water's edge.

Outdoor Adventures:
Adventure seekers will find a plethora of activities to indulge in on the Isle of Skye. Hiking and trekking are at the forefront, with trails catering to all levels of expertise. The Cuillin Mountains, with their challenging peaks and ridges, are a mecca for experienced climbers. The less strenuous walks offer equally rewarding experiences, such as the enchanting Fairy Glen or the coastal path from Elgol to Loch Coruisk.

Water sports enthusiasts can explore the coastline by kayaking or enjoy fishing in the island's pristine waters. Wildlife spotting is also a popular activity, with opportunities to observe seals, dolphins, and a variety of bird species in their natural habitat.

Cultural Treasures:
Beyond its natural wonders, Skye is steeped in history and culture. The island's Gaelic heritage is preserved through its language, music, and traditional festivities. Visit the Skye Museum of Island Life to gain insights into the lives of the island's past inhabitants, or explore Dunvegan Castle, the oldest continuously inhabited castle in Scotland, which offers a glimpse into the history of the MacLeod clan.

Local Cuisine:
Indulge in the island's local cuisine, which emphasizes fresh seafood and locally sourced ingredients. Feast on succulent scallops, mouthwatering langoustines, and delectable smoked salmon. The island's vibrant food scene also includes charming cafes, pubs, and restaurants that serve both traditional and modern Scottish dishes.

Planning Your Trip:

Consider visiting Skye during the warmer months, from spring to early autumn, to make the most of outdoor activities and to witness the island's natural beauty in full bloom. Accommodation options range from quaint bed and breakfasts to charming cottages and luxury lodges, many of which offer stunning views of the surrounding landscapes.

The Isle of Skye is a realm of natural wonders and outdoor adventures that will leave you spellbound. With its breathtaking landscapes, diverse activities, and rich cultural heritage, Skye is an idyllic destination for those seeking to immerse themselves in the beauty and serenity of the Scottish wilderness. Whether you're a nature lover, an adventure enthusiast, or a cultural explorer, the Isle of Skye promises an unforgettable journey that captures the heart and soul of Scotland's untamed beauty.

3.5 Loch Ness: Mythical Legends and Scenic Cruises

Welcome to the legendary shores of Loch Ness, a place where myth and mystery intertwine with stunning natural beauty. Nestled in the heart of the Scottish Highlands, Loch Ness is famous not only for its breathtaking landscapes but also for the elusive creature said to inhabit its depths. This travel guide will take you on a journey through the mythical legends, scenic cruises, and captivating experiences that Loch Ness has to offer.

Mythical Legends:

No discussion of Loch Ness is complete without mentioning the legendary creature known as the Loch Ness Monster, affectionately called "Nessie." The tales of Nessie's presence in the waters of the loch have captured the imagination of people from around the world. Whether you're a true believer or a skeptic, the mystery and allure of Nessie remain an integral part of Loch Ness's identity.

Local legends recount sightings of a serpentine creature with humps, a long neck, and a head emerging from the water. The mystery has fueled expeditions, investigations, and scientific research, making Loch Ness a truly fascinating destination for those intrigued by the unknown.

Scenic Cruises:

One of the best ways to experience the majesty of Loch Ness is by embarking on a scenic cruise across its dark and tranquil waters. Cruise operators offer a variety of options, from leisurely day cruises to twilight excursions that add an air of mystique to the experience.

As you glide across the loch's surface, you'll be treated to panoramic views of the surrounding hills and forests. The stillness of the water contrasts with the grandeur of the landscape, creating an ambiance of serenity that's truly magical. And who knows, you might even catch a glimpse of Nessie, if luck is on your side!

Historic Sites:
Loch Ness is also home to several historic sites that add to its allure. Urquhart Castle, perched on the shores of the loch, offers a glimpse into Scotland's turbulent past. Explore the ruins, climb the Grant Tower for a stunning view, and learn about the castle's rich history through interactive displays.

Outdoor Activities:
Beyond the myths and legends, Loch Ness offers a range of outdoor activities. Hiking trails along the loch's shoreline provide opportunities to appreciate the beauty of the landscape up close. The Great Glen Way, a long-distance footpath, meanders through charming villages and offers captivating vistas of the loch.

Fishing enthusiasts can try their luck in Loch Ness's deep and mysterious waters, while cyclists can explore the scenic trails that wind through the surrounding hills and forests.

Local Cuisine:
After a day of exploration, indulge in the local cuisine that celebrates Scotland's culinary traditions. Sample dishes such as Cullen skink, a hearty smoked haddock soup, or enjoy freshly caught seafood. Pair your meal with a glass of Scotch whisky for a truly authentic experience.

Planning Your Trip:
Consider visiting Loch Ness during the warmer months, from spring to autumn, when the weather is more favorable for outdoor activities and scenic cruises. Accommodation options range from cozy bed and breakfasts to charming lodges, many of which offer views of the loch.

Loch Ness is a destination that embraces both the mystical and the natural. Whether you're drawn by the legends of Nessie, the serene beauty of the loch, or the historic sites that dot its shores, Loch Ness promises an unforgettable journey that will leave you enchanted and inspired by the magic of Scotland's Highlands.

3.6 Stirling: Historic Battlefields and Medieval Architecture

Step into the pages of history as you explore the captivating city of Stirling, nestled in the heart of Scotland. With its rich heritage, historic battlefields, and stunning medieval architecture, Stirling is a treasure trove for history enthusiasts and travelers seeking a glimpse into Scotland's past. This travel guide will take you on a journey through the city's iconic battlefields, majestic castles, and captivating heritage.

Historic Battlefields:

Stirling's significance in Scottish history is deeply rooted in its historic battlefields. The Battle of Stirling Bridge, fought in 1297, marked a turning point in the Scottish Wars of Independence. Led by William Wallace, the Scottish forces achieved a remarkable victory against the English army. The National Wallace Monument stands as a tribute to Wallace's bravery and offers panoramic views of the surrounding landscape.

Another significant battle took place in 1314 at the Battle of Bannockburn. Here, Scottish King Robert the Bruce led his forces to a resounding victory against the English, solidifying Scotland's independence. The Bannockburn Heritage Centre provides an immersive experience that transports visitors back to this pivotal moment in history.

Medieval Architecture:
Stirling's historic charm is reflected in its medieval architecture, which transports visitors back in time. Stirling Castle, perched atop Castle Hill, is a true architectural gem. The castle's grandeur and strategic importance have made it a key player in Scotland's history. Explore its regal halls, intricate tapestries, and beautifully restored Great Hall, and be sure to take in the breathtaking views of the city and surrounding countryside.

The Church of the Holy Rude, adjacent to the castle, is another architectural marvel. With its intricate stained glass windows and centuries-old ambiance, the church provides insight into Scotland's religious history.

Cultural Treasures:
Stirling's vibrant culture is also evident in its museums and galleries. The Smith Art Gallery and Museum showcases an impressive collection of art, artifacts, and historical exhibits that highlight the city's heritage. The Stirling Old Town Jail provides a glimpse into the lives of prisoners from a bygone

era and offers interactive exhibits that engage visitors of all ages.

Outdoor Activities:
The surrounding landscapes offer opportunities for outdoor exploration. The Ochil Hills provide scenic hiking trails with panoramic views, while the Forth River offers canoeing and kayaking adventures. The Stirling Ghostwalk is a unique way to learn about the city's history and folklore as you stroll through its historic streets.

Local Cuisine:
Stirling's culinary scene blends traditional Scottish fare with modern flavors. Savor dishes like haggis, neeps and tatties, or enjoy a hearty pub meal. Don't forget to try local delicacies like Stornoway black pudding and cranachan, a delicious dessert made with raspberries, cream, oats, and whisky.

Planning Your Trip:
Stirling can be enjoyed year-round, with milder weather during spring and summer. The city offers a range of accommodations, from charming bed and breakfasts to boutique hotels, often with views of the castle or historic sites.

Stirling is a city where history comes alive, where battles were fought and castles were built, shaping Scotland's identity and resilience. Whether you're captivated by historic battlefields, medieval architecture, or cultural treasures, Stirling promises an immersive journey that will transport you through time and leave you with a deeper appreciation for Scotland's rich past.

3.7 Aberdeen: Coastal Gems and Whisky Trails

Welcome to Aberdeen, a vibrant city nestled along the stunning coastline of Scotland. Known for its coastal beauty, historic charm, and connections to the world of whisky, Aberdeen offers a unique blend of experiences for travelers. This travel guide will take you on a journey through the city's coastal gems, historic sites, and the whisky trails that make Aberdeen a must-visit destination.

Coastal Gems:
Aberdeen's coastline is a tapestry of rugged cliffs, golden beaches, and charming fishing villages. The dramatic contrasts between the North Sea's waves and the tranquility of the shoreline create a captivating ambiance. The Beach Promenade is a favorite spot for locals and visitors alike, offering

leisurely strolls, stunning sunsets, and a chance to breathe in the fresh sea air.

Just a short drive from the city, you'll find picturesque villages such as Stonehaven, known for its historic harbor and the stunning Dunnottar Castle perched dramatically atop a cliff. Further north lies Cruden Bay, where the ruins of Slains Castle overlook the North Sea, providing a scene of haunting beauty.

Historic Sites:
Aberdeen boasts a rich history, evident in its historic sites and architecture. The medieval St. Machar's Cathedral, with its intricate stained glass windows and stunning ceiling, showcases the city's ecclesiastical heritage. The 16th-century Provost Skene's House offers a glimpse into Aberdeen's past through its period rooms and exhibits.

Marischal College, a striking granite building, stands as one of the world's largest granite structures and a symbol of the city's grandeur. Take a walk along the cobbled streets of Old Aberdeen to admire well-preserved buildings and immerse yourself in the ambiance of centuries gone by.

Whisky Trails:

Aberdeen is a gateway to Scotland's whisky heritage. The region is home to several distilleries that produce some of the finest Scotch whiskies. Embark on a whisky trail to explore the craft and tradition behind this beloved spirit.

The Malt Whisky Trail takes you through the picturesque Speyside region, where you can visit renowned distilleries like Glenfiddich and Macallan. You'll gain insights into the whisky-making process, learn about the history of each distillery, and have the opportunity to sample a dram or two.

Local Cuisine:
Aberdeen's culinary scene is as diverse as its landscape. Fresh seafood takes center stage, with the city's coastal location providing a steady supply of delights like lobster, crab, and North Sea haddock. Enjoy a traditional fish supper from a local chippy or dine in one of the city's many restaurants offering contemporary Scottish cuisine.

Outdoor Adventures:
Outdoor enthusiasts will find ample opportunities for adventure around Aberdeen. The Cairngorms National Park is within driving distance, offering hiking, cycling, and winter sports. If golf is your

passion, don't miss the chance to play on one of the area's scenic golf courses.

Planning Your Trip:

Aberdeen experiences milder weather during the summer months, making it an ideal time to explore its outdoor attractions and coastal beauty. The city offers a range of accommodations, from boutique hotels to cozy bed and breakfasts, providing options for every traveler's preference.

Aberdeen is a city that delights the senses, with its coastal allure, historic charm, and whisky heritage. Whether you're captivated by the beauty of the coastline, the richness of history, or the world of whisky, Aberdeen promises an unforgettable journey that captures the essence of Scotland's diverse and captivating spirit.

CHAPTER 4. Family-Friendly Activities and Attractions

4.1 Edinburgh Castle: A Fascinating History Lesson

Welcome to Edinburgh Castle, a historic fortress that stands proudly atop Castle Rock, overlooking the enchanting city of Edinburgh. With its rich history, breathtaking architecture, and commanding presence, Edinburgh Castle is a must-visit destination for travelers seeking a captivating journey through Scotland's past. This travel guide will take you on an immersive tour of the castle, offering insights into its fascinating history and significance.

Historic Significance:
Edinburgh Castle holds a prominent place in Scotland's history, having witnessed centuries of royal ceremonies, military conflicts, and cultural developments. The castle's strategic location made it a stronghold for both defensive and symbolic purposes, serving as a symbol of power and sovereignty.

Historical Highlights:
Explore the Great Hall, where Scottish kings and queens hosted grand banquets and celebrations.

The Crown Jewels of Scotland, including the iconic Crown, Sceptre, and Sword of State, are on display, representing the nation's regal heritage.

Don't miss the Stone of Destiny, a symbol of Scottish kingship for centuries. The Scottish National War Memorial pays tribute to those who gave their lives in various conflicts, while the St. Margaret's Chapel, dating back to the 12th century, offers a serene escape within the castle walls.

One O'Clock Gun:
Experience the firing of the One O'Clock Gun, a tradition that dates back to 1861. Originally intended to help ships in the Firth of Forth set their maritime clocks, the daily firing of the gun continues to be a popular attraction for visitors and locals alike.

Mons Meg:
Marvel at Mons Meg, a medieval bombard that played a crucial role in historic battles. Its massive size and historical significance make it a captivating relic of medieval warfare.

Panoramic Views:
Apart from its historical treasures, Edinburgh Castle offers breathtaking panoramic views of the

city and its surroundings. The sweeping vistas from the castle walls allow you to appreciate the architectural beauty of the city while taking in the natural splendor of the landscape.

The Honours of Scotland:
Discover the Honours of Scotland, also known as the Scottish Crown Jewels. These precious artifacts include the Crown, Sceptre, and Sword of State, symbolizing the sovereignty of the Scottish nation.

Interactive Exhibits:
Edinburgh Castle's interactive exhibits use cutting-edge technology to bring history to life. Virtual tours, immersive displays, and multimedia presentations offer a dynamic and engaging learning experience for visitors of all ages.

Planning Your Visit:
Consider visiting Edinburgh Castle during the morning or early afternoon to avoid crowds. The castle is open year-round, and you can check the official website for up-to-date information on opening hours, tickets, and any special events.

Edinburgh Castle is not just a monument; it's a living testament to the rich tapestry of Scotland's history. From its royal chambers to its military fortifications, the castle offers a captivating journey through time, providing a window into the struggles, triumphs, and evolution of the nation. Whether you're a history enthusiast or simply seeking to immerse yourself in Scotland's cultural heritage, Edinburgh Castle promises an unforgettable experience that will leave you awed and inspired.

4.2 Dynamic Earth: Interactive Science Museum

Welcome to Dynamic Earth, an awe-inspiring interactive science museum located in Edinburgh, Scotland. As a visitor, you'll embark on a journey through time, space, and the natural world, all while engaging in hands-on experiences that make learning an exciting adventure. This travel guide will introduce you to the wonders of Dynamic Earth and provide insights into the captivating experiences that await.

A Journey Through Time:
Dynamic Earth takes you on a journey spanning over 4.6 billion years of Earth's history. From the Big Bang that initiated the universe to the emergence of life and the shaping of our planet, the exhibits provide a comprehensive overview of the Earth's evolution.

Interactive Exhibits:
One of the highlights of Dynamic Earth is its interactive exhibits that engage visitors of all ages. Walk through the Time Machine, a simulated time-travel experience that transports you to key moments in Earth's history. Experience earthquakes, volcanic eruptions, and other natural phenomena in the Earthquake Café, an earthquake simulator that immerses you in the power of the planet's forces.

Ice Age to Climate Change:
Explore the Ice Age and witness the effects of changing temperatures on the Earth's landscapes. Learn about climate change, its causes, and its impact on the planet through captivating displays and informative exhibits.

The Ozone Zone:
Step into the Ozone Zone to discover the science behind the ozone layer, its importance in protecting life on Earth, and the challenges it faces due to human activities.

The ShowDome:
The ShowDome is an immersive cinema where you can enjoy spectacular shows that explore various

aspects of Earth and space science. From journeys through the cosmos to underwater adventures, the ShowDome offers a unique and mesmerizing experience.

Outdoor Spaces:
Dynamic Earth isn't just confined to indoor exhibits. The outdoor spaces include a tranquil courtyard and a unique landscape that reflects Scotland's geological diversity. Enjoy a leisurely stroll while taking in the beauty of the surroundings.

Education and Learning:
Dynamic Earth offers educational programs tailored to different age groups, making it an ideal destination for school trips and family outings. The hands-on experiences and interactive displays make learning about science an engaging and enjoyable endeavor.

Visitor Facilities:
The museum features a café where you can enjoy refreshments and meals while overlooking the stunning Salisbury Crags. The gift shop offers a variety of science-themed souvenirs, books, and educational materials.

Planning Your Visit:
Check the museum's official website for information on opening hours, ticket prices, and any special events or exhibitions. Dynamic Earth is located near the city center of Edinburgh, making it easily accessible for both local residents and tourists.

Dynamic Earth isn't just a museum; it's an immersive journey that ignites curiosity and fuels a passion for science. With its interactive exhibits, engaging displays, and a commitment to educational excellence, the museum provides an experience that's as entertaining as it is enlightening. Whether you're traveling with family, friends, or as a solo explorer, Dynamic Earth promises a captivating adventure that will leave you inspired by the wonders of our planet and the universe beyond.

4.3 Highland Wildlife Park: Encounter Native Wildlife

Welcome to the Highland Wildlife Park, a unique destination that allows you to get up close and personal with Scotland's native and exotic wildlife. Located in the stunning Cairngorms National Park, this park offers a captivating experience where conservation, education, and exploration come together. This travel guide will introduce you to the wonders of the Highland Wildlife Park and provide insights into the exciting encounters that await.

Native and Exotic Wildlife:
The Highland Wildlife Park is home to a diverse range of animals, both native to Scotland and from around the world. From European bison and red deer to Amur tigers and snow leopards, the park provides a safe and natural habitat for these magnificent creatures.

Safari Experience:
Embark on a safari adventure through the park's large open enclosures. Observe animals like European elk, Przewalski's horses, and wild boars as they roam freely in surroundings that mimic their natural habitats. The safari experience gives you a rare opportunity to see these animals in a more natural setting than traditional zoos.

Polar Bears and Arctic Tundra:
One of the highlights of the park is its polar bear enclosure, which features a tundra-like environment that resembles the Arctic. Observe these majestic bears as they swim, play, and interact in a space designed to mimic their native habitat.

Red Pandas and Snow Leopards:
The park is home to some of the world's most
endangered species, including red pandas and snow
leopards. Witness these elusive creatures in
habitats carefully designed to meet their needs and
ensure their well-being.

Encounters and Keeper Talks:
Highland Wildlife Park offers a range of encounters
and keeper talks that provide deeper insights into
the animals' lives and behaviors. Join a keeper talk
to learn about the park's conservation efforts, the
challenges faced by different species, and the role of
the park in preserving biodiversity.

Wildlife Breeding and Conservation:
The park is actively involved in breeding programs
for endangered species, contributing to global
conservation efforts. Your visit helps support these
initiatives and raises awareness about the
importance of protecting wildlife and their habitats.

Outdoor Play Areas:
The park is family-friendly, with outdoor play areas
where children can have fun and learn about
wildlife simultaneously. Adventure playgrounds,
nature trails, and picnic spots provide opportunities

for families to enjoy quality time in a natural setting.

Visitor Facilities:
The park features a café where you can enjoy refreshments and meals, as well as a gift shop offering a variety of wildlife-themed souvenirs and educational materials.

Planning Your Visit:
Check the park's official website for information on opening hours, ticket prices, and any special events or programs. The park is easily accessible from Aviemore and Inverness, making it a convenient destination for tourists and local visitors alike.

The Highland Wildlife Park is a sanctuary of wonder, where you can connect with native wildlife and exotic creatures in a natural and respectful environment. Whether you're a nature enthusiast, a family looking for an educational outing, or simply someone who wants to experience the magic of animals up close, the Highland Wildlife Park promises an unforgettable adventure that will leave you inspired by the beauty and diversity of our planet's wildlife.

4.4 Blair Drummond Safari Park: An African Adventure

Welcome to Blair Drummond Safari Park, a captivating destination that transports you to the wilds of Africa without leaving Scotland. Located near Stirling, this park offers a unique opportunity to get up close and personal with a diverse range of animals from around the world. From safari drives to animal encounters, this travel guide will introduce you to the wonders of Blair Drummond Safari Park and provide insights into the exciting experiences that await.

Safari Drive:
Embark on an unforgettable safari drive through open enclosures that mimic the natural habitats of animals from different continents. From lions and tigers to rhinos and elephants, the safari drive allows you to observe these magnificent creatures as they roam freely and exhibit their natural behaviors.

African Safari:
Experience an African adventure in the heart of Scotland as you encounter giraffes, zebras, and antelopes on the savannah. Witness the grace and beauty of these animals as they graze and interact

in a landscape that transports you to the African plains.

Monkey Jungle and Lemur Land:
Blair Drummond Safari Park is home to a variety of primates. Wander through the Monkey Jungle and observe playful macaques and capuchins as they swing through the trees. In Lemur Land, get an up-close look at ring-tailed lemurs and red ruffed lemurs in a habitat that replicates their natural surroundings.

Sea Lion Presentation:
Don't miss the sea lion presentation, where these charismatic marine mammals showcase their intelligence and agility. Learn about their behaviors, natural habitats, and the conservation efforts aimed at protecting their species.

Animal Encounters:
Blair Drummond Safari Park offers a range of animal encounters that allow you to interact with some of the park's residents. From feeding giraffes and lemurs to meeting reptiles and creepy crawlies, these encounters provide educational insights and memorable experiences.

Adventure Playground and Pedal Boats:

The park features an adventure playground where children can burn off energy and have fun. Additionally, the pedal boats on the park's loch offer a relaxing activity that provides a unique perspective of the surroundings.

Keeper Talks and Shows:
Join keeper talks and shows to learn more about the animals' lives, behaviors, and conservation efforts. These presentations offer fascinating insights into the species that call Blair Drummond Safari Park home.

Conservation Initiatives:
The park actively participates in conservation programs to protect endangered species and support wildlife conservation efforts worldwide. Your visit contributes to these initiatives and raises awareness about the importance of safeguarding biodiversity.

Visitor Facilities:
Blair Drummond Safari Park offers facilities including cafés and picnic areas, allowing you to enjoy refreshments or meals while surrounded by the park's natural beauty. The gift shop offers a variety of souvenirs, toys, and educational materials.

Planning Your Visit:
Check the park's official website for information on opening hours, ticket prices, and any special events or programs. The park is easily accessible from Stirling and surrounding areas.

Blair Drummond Safari Park offers a thrilling African adventure in the heart of Scotland, where you can encounter exotic animals and learn about their lives and habitats. Whether you're seeking a family-friendly outing, a chance to connect with wildlife, or an educational experience, the park promises an unforgettable journey that will leave you inspired by the diversity and wonder of the animal kingdom.

4.5 Loch Lomond Shores: Waterfront Fun and Activities

Welcome to Loch Lomond Shores, a picturesque waterfront destination that offers a blend of natural beauty, outdoor activities, and leisurely pursuits. Nestled on the shores of Loch Lomond, the largest freshwater lake in Great Britain, this location provides a unique opportunity to enjoy the splendor of the Scottish countryside. This travel guide will introduce you to the charms of Loch Lomond

Shores and provide insights into the exciting experiences that await.

Stunning Loch Views:
Loch Lomond Shores offers panoramic views of Loch Lomond's glistening waters and the surrounding hills. The beauty of the landscape creates a serene ambiance that invites relaxation and exploration.

Shopping and Dining:
The complex features a variety of shops, boutiques, and galleries where you can shop for local crafts, artwork, and souvenirs. The area also offers a selection of cafes and restaurants, allowing you to enjoy a meal with a backdrop of breathtaking loch views.

Outdoor Activities:
Loch Lomond Shores caters to outdoor enthusiasts of all ages. The expansive outdoor spaces provide opportunities for leisurely walks, picnics, and enjoying the fresh air. For those seeking adventure, the area offers water sports, hiking, and cycling.

Sea Life Centre:
Discover the wonders of underwater life at the Loch Lomond SEA LIFE Centre. Explore themed tanks

showcasing a variety of marine creatures, from seahorses and rays to sharks and turtles. The interactive exhibits and touch pools offer an engaging educational experience for visitors of all ages.

Loch Cruises:
Experience the beauty of Loch Lomond up close by taking a leisurely cruise on the water. Cruises range from short trips to longer excursions, allowing you to appreciate the loch's tranquility while soaking in the scenic vistas.

Bird of Prey Centre:
The Bird of Prey Centre at Loch Lomond Shores provides an opportunity to get acquainted with majestic raptors. Watch awe-inspiring displays featuring falcons, eagles, and owls as they showcase their natural hunting and flying abilities.

Family-Friendly Activities:
Loch Lomond Shores is perfect for families, offering activities such as adventure golf, a play park, and a miniature railway. The kid-friendly attractions ensure that visitors of all ages have a memorable and enjoyable experience.

Festivals and Events:

Throughout the year, Loch Lomond Shores hosts a variety of festivals, events, and markets. These provide an opportunity to experience the local culture, sample delicious food, and shop for unique products.

Visitor Facilities:
Loch Lomond Shores offers visitor facilities including parking, restrooms, and information centers. The area is designed to accommodate the needs of both locals and tourists.

Planning Your Visit:
Check the official website of Loch Lomond Shores for information on opening hours, event schedules, and any special activities. The destination is easily accessible from Glasgow and surrounding areas.

Loch Lomond Shores is a haven of natural beauty and recreational opportunities, offering a delightful blend of relaxation and adventure. Whether you're seeking a serene lakeside experience, family-friendly fun, or a chance to explore the loch's waters, Loch Lomond Shores promises an unforgettable journey that will leave you inspired by the allure of Scotland's stunning landscapes.

4.6 Fairy Pools on the Isle of Skye: Enchanting Hike for Kids

Welcome to the enchanting Fairy Pools on the Isle of Skye, a magical destination that promises a memorable outdoor adventure for families with kids. Nestled amidst the breathtaking landscapes of the Scottish Highlands, the Fairy Pools offer a captivating hike that allows children to explore nature's wonders while sparking their imagination. This travel guide will introduce you to the beauty of the Fairy Pools and provide insights into the enchanting experience that awaits young explorers.

A Whimsical Landscape:
The Fairy Pools are a series of crystal-clear pools and waterfalls, set against a backdrop of stunning hills and rugged terrain. The name "Fairy Pools" is derived from the mystical aura of the place, where the sparkling waters and vibrant hues create an otherworldly ambiance that ignites the imagination.

Family-Friendly Hike:
The hike to the Fairy Pools is family-friendly and suitable for kids of varying ages. The trail is relatively easy, making it an excellent opportunity for children to experience the joy of outdoor exploration. The distance and terrain are

manageable, allowing families to go at their own pace and take breaks when needed.

Natural Playgrounds:
Along the hike, kids will encounter natural playgrounds created by the elements. Large rocks, fallen trees, and shallow streams offer opportunities for climbing, balancing, and imaginative play. These natural features add an element of excitement and engagement to the journey.

Splash and Play:
As you progress along the trail, you'll encounter a series of pools and waterfalls. Children can dip their feet in the cool waters, skip stones, and enjoy the thrill of splashing around. The Fairy Pools provide a safe and picturesque environment for kids to interact with nature.

Imagination and Folklore:
The magical atmosphere of the Fairy Pools lends itself to storytelling and imaginative play. Encourage kids to envision the realm of fairies and mythical creatures as they explore this enchanting landscape. The cascading waterfalls and hidden nooks offer the perfect backdrop for weaving tales of adventure and magic.

Safety and Considerations:
While the Fairy Pools hike is family-friendly, it's essential to prioritize safety. Make sure kids are dressed appropriately for outdoor activities, with sturdy footwear and weather-appropriate clothing. Bring snacks, water, and any necessary supplies for a comfortable hike. Be mindful of the terrain and supervise children near water bodies.

Planning Your Visit:
The best time to visit the Fairy Pools is during the warmer months, from spring to early autumn, when the weather is more favorable for outdoor activities. Check weather conditions before heading out and consider the availability of parking, as the Fairy Pools are a popular destination.

The Fairy Pools on the Isle of Skye offer a truly enchanting experience for families with kids, where imagination, exploration, and the beauty of nature converge. The hike's accessibility, natural play opportunities, and the allure of the landscape make it an ideal destination for young adventurers. Whether you're splashing in the pools, weaving tales of fairies, or simply enjoying quality time outdoors, the Fairy Pools promise a memorable journey that will create lasting memories for both kids and parents alike.

4.7 Kelvingrove Art Gallery and Museum: Engaging Exhibits

Welcome to the Kelvingrove Art Gallery and Museum, a cultural gem nestled in the vibrant city of Glasgow, Scotland. With its diverse collection, captivating exhibits, and stunning architecture, Kelvingrove offers a rich and engaging experience for art enthusiasts, history buffs, and curious visitors of all ages. This travel guide will introduce you to the wonders of Kelvingrove and provide insights into the exciting exhibits that await your exploration.

A Historic Landmark:

Kelvingrove Art Gallery and Museum is not only a treasure trove of art and artifacts but also an architectural marvel. The grand Victorian building's red sandstone facade and intricate design make it an iconic landmark that exudes elegance and grandeur.

Diverse Collections:

The museum's vast collection spans art, history, and natural history. From ancient artifacts and European paintings to interactive displays and dinosaur skeletons, Kelvingrove's diverse offerings cater to a wide range of interests.

European Art:
Kelvingrove boasts an impressive collection of European art, featuring works from various periods and styles. Discover paintings by renowned artists such as Rembrandt, Van Gogh, and Botticelli, providing a journey through the evolution of artistic expression.

Scottish Art and History:
Explore the history and culture of Scotland through its art and artifacts. Learn about the country's rich heritage, from medieval times to the present day, through exhibits that showcase Scottish identity, traditions, and achievements.

Natural History and Science:
Kelvingrove's natural history section includes everything from fossils and minerals to taxidermy animals and interactive displays. The museum's focus on science and natural history provides an educational and entertaining experience for visitors of all ages.

Charles Rennie Mackintosh and Glasgow Style:
Discover the works of renowned architect and designer Charles Rennie Mackintosh, a figure who played a significant role in shaping Glasgow's art

scene. Kelvingrove features a dedicated section that celebrates the Glasgow Style and showcases Mackintosh's innovative designs.

Interactive Displays:
Engaging and interactive displays are a hallmark of Kelvingrove. From virtual reality experiences to touch-screen exhibits, the museum employs technology to enhance the visitor's understanding and appreciation of the collections.

Organ Concerts:
The organ in Kelvingrove's main hall is an attraction in itself. Don't miss the opportunity to attend one of the regular organ concerts, where the majestic instrument fills the gallery with beautiful music, creating an immersive experience.

Visitor Facilities:
The museum features facilities such as a café and gift shop, allowing visitors to enjoy refreshments and shop for unique souvenirs and art-related merchandise.

Planning Your Visit:
Kelvingrove Art Gallery and Museum is easily accessible in the heart of Glasgow. Check the museum's official website for information on

opening hours, special exhibitions, and any events or guided tours that might be available.

Kelvingrove Art Gallery and Museum is a captivating destination that offers an immersive journey through art, history, and culture. Whether you're an art enthusiast, history buff, or simply seeking an enriching experience, Kelvingrove promises an unforgettable exploration of diverse collections, interactive exhibits, and the beauty of human creativity. With its stunning architecture and engaging displays, Kelvingrove invites you to embark on a cultural adventure that will leave you inspired and enlightened.

CHAPTER 5. Romantic Escapes for Couples

5.1 Romantic Strolls in Edinburgh's Old Town

Welcome to the charming and historic Old Town of Edinburgh, Scotland. With its cobbled streets, medieval architecture, and romantic ambiance, the Old Town provides the perfect setting for leisurely and enchanting strolls with your loved one. This travel guide will take you on a journey through the romantic alleys, hidden courtyards, and iconic landmarks that make Edinburgh's Old Town a haven for couples seeking a romantic escape.

Cobblestone Streets and Medieval Charm:
Step back in time as you wander through the narrow and winding cobblestone streets of the Old Town. The medieval architecture, centuries-old buildings, and intricate details create an atmosphere that transports you to a bygone era, making every step a romantic journey through history.

The Royal Mile:
Begin your romantic stroll on the Royal Mile, the main thoroughfare of the Old Town. Lined with shops, cafes, and historic sites, the Royal Mile is a

bustling yet captivating street that offers a mix of vibrant activity and a sense of old-world charm.

St. Giles' Cathedral:
Pause to admire St. Giles' Cathedral, a stunning Gothic masterpiece that has witnessed countless weddings, ceremonies, and historic events. The intricate architecture and beautiful stained glass windows provide a serene and romantic backdrop.

Hidden Courtyards and Gardens:
Explore hidden courtyards and secret gardens that provide moments of tranquility amidst the urban bustle. Dunbar's Close Garden, a secluded green oasis, offers a quiet place to unwind and enjoy each other's company.

The Real Mary King's Close:
For a unique experience, consider a tour of The Real Mary King's Close, a series of underground streets and spaces that reveal the city's history and stories. This immersive adventure allows you to explore hidden corners and learn about the lives of Edinburgh's past residents.

Edinburgh Castle:
As you continue your stroll, you'll be treated to captivating glimpses of Edinburgh Castle atop

Castle Rock. The castle's illuminated silhouette against the night sky creates a truly romantic sight, especially as the sun sets over the city.

Calton Hill:
For panoramic views and a touch of romance, make your way to Calton Hill. A short climb rewards you with breathtaking vistas of the city, the sea, and the surrounding landscapes. This vantage point is especially captivating during sunrise or sunset.

Candlelit Dinners:
After your romantic stroll, indulge in a candlelit dinner at one of the charming restaurants in the Old Town. Enjoying a traditional Scottish meal or international cuisine while basking in the historic ambiance is the perfect way to conclude your evening.

Planning Your Romantic Stroll:
Edinburgh's Old Town is accessible year-round, and the best time for a romantic stroll is during the quieter hours of the evening, when the streets are lit and the city takes on a magical glow. Wear comfortable shoes for walking on cobblestones and be sure to check the opening hours of any attractions you plan to visit.

Edinburgh's Old Town offers couples a romantic and captivating experience that weaves together history, architecture, and enchanting moments. Whether you're wandering down ancient streets, exploring hidden gardens, or gazing upon iconic landmarks, the Old Town invites you to create cherished memories and celebrate the beauty of love in a setting steeped in history and charm.

5.2 Loch Lomond Boat Cruises: Scenic Serenity

Welcome to the serene beauty of Loch Lomond, Scotland's largest freshwater lake. One of the best ways to truly experience the majesty of this iconic loch is by embarking on a boat cruise. Loch Lomond boat cruises offer a unique opportunity to immerse yourself in the breathtaking landscapes, tranquil waters, and surrounding nature. This travel guide will take you on a journey through the serene beauty of Loch Lomond and provide insights into the enchanting experience that awaits you on a boat cruise.

The Beauty of Loch Lomond:
Loch Lomond is renowned for its stunning natural beauty, encompassing serene waters, lush forests, and rolling hills. The loch is framed by the Trossachs National Park, an area of outstanding

natural beauty that offers a sense of tranquility and a chance to escape the hustle and bustle of everyday life.

Types of Boat Cruises:
Loch Lomond offers a variety of boat cruises to cater to different preferences and interests. Whether you're seeking a leisurely sightseeing experience, a romantic outing, or an informative guided tour, there's a cruise that suits your desires.

Scenic Sightseeing:
Sightseeing cruises are perfect for those who want to sit back, relax, and take in the stunning landscapes. These cruises provide an opportunity to admire the loch's picturesque islands, serene waters, and the backdrop of the surrounding mountains.

Guided Tours:
Guided boat cruises offer an educational and informative experience. Knowledgeable guides share insights about the history, geology, and local wildlife of Loch Lomond, adding depth to your journey and enhancing your connection with the surroundings.

Island Exploration:

Some cruises include stops at one or more of Loch Lomond's islands. These stops allow you to disembark, explore the islands' natural beauty, and enjoy a peaceful walk before rejoining the cruise.

Sunset Cruises:
For a touch of romance and magic, consider a sunset cruise. As the sun dips below the horizon, the loch's tranquil waters reflect the warm hues of the sky, creating an unforgettable and serene atmosphere.

Wildlife Encounters:
Keep an eye out for the diverse wildlife that calls Loch Lomond home. Ospreys, golden eagles, red deer, and various waterfowl are among the creatures that may make an appearance during your cruise.

Photography Opportunities:
The picturesque landscapes and ever-changing light conditions make Loch Lomond a paradise for photographers. Capture the reflections on the water, the play of light on the hills, and the loch's serene beauty.

Planning Your Cruise:

Boat cruises on Loch Lomond operate seasonally, usually from spring to autumn. Check the schedules and availability of different cruises before your visit. Dress comfortably and consider bringing a light jacket, as the weather near the water can be cooler than on land.

Loch Lomond boat cruises offer a serene and captivating experience that allows you to connect with nature, unwind, and immerse yourself in the breathtaking beauty of the Scottish Highlands. Whether you're enjoying the scenic vistas, learning about the loch's history, or simply savoring the peaceful moments, a boat cruise on Loch Lomond promises an unforgettable journey that captures the essence of Scotland's natural splendor.

5.3 Whisky Distillery Tours: Intimate Tastings

Welcome to the heart of Scotland's whisky culture, where centuries of tradition and craftsmanship come together to produce one of the world's most beloved spirits. Whisky distillery tours offer an intimate and immersive experience that takes you behind the scenes of whisky production, introduces you to the art of distilling, and culminates in the joy of tasting this iconic drink. This travel guide will lead you through the enchanting world of whisky distillery tours, providing insights into the process, the culture, and the memorable tastings that await.

A Spirit of Tradition:
Whisky, often referred to as "the water of life," is deeply woven into Scotland's cultural fabric. The distillation of whisky has been practiced for centuries, with each distillery carrying its own traditions, techniques, and unique flavors.

Types of Distillery Tours:
Whisky distillery tours cater to a range of preferences, from beginners curious about the process to connoisseurs seeking to deepen their knowledge. There are various types of tours, each offering a distinct perspective on whisky production.

Guided Tours:
Guided tours provide a comprehensive overview of the whisky-making process. Expert guides walk you through each step, from mashing and fermentation to distillation and maturation. Learn about the ingredients, the role of different types of casks, and the science behind the flavors.

Private Tours:

For a more personalized experience, some distilleries offer private tours. These exclusive tours often include access to areas not open to the public and allow for in-depth conversations with knowledgeable staff.

Tasting Sessions:
Tasting sessions are the highlight of any distillery tour. Learn how to appreciate the aroma, color, and palate of different whisky varieties. Expert guides will help you distinguish between the subtle flavors and complexities that make each whisky unique.

Whisky and Food Pairings:
Some distilleries offer whisky and food pairing experiences, where you can explore how different whiskies complement various flavors. These sessions enhance your understanding of whisky's versatility and its ability to elevate culinary experiences.

Exploring Different Regions:
Scotland's whisky production is divided into distinct regions, each with its own characteristics. From the peaty and smoky whiskies of Islay to the smooth and honeyed notes of the Highlands, exploring different regions allows you to discover a wide spectrum of flavors.

Immerse in Local Culture:
Whisky distilleries are often located in picturesque landscapes and quaint villages. Visiting a distillery allows you to immerse yourself in the local culture, interact with passionate locals, and gain a deeper understanding of the community's connection to whisky.

Collecting Souvenirs:
Most distilleries have well-stocked shops where you can purchase a variety of whisky-related souvenirs, from bottles of their finest creations to branded glassware and accessories.

Planning Your Distillery Tour:
Before embarking on a whisky distillery tour, research the distilleries you'd like to visit, as each offers a unique experience. Check their websites for tour availability, schedules, and any COVID-19-related guidelines. Consider booking in advance, especially during peak tourist seasons.

Whisky distillery tours are a journey into the heart and soul of Scotland's whisky-making heritage. From the aromatic mashes to the amber nectar in your glass, these tours offer a deep appreciation for the craftsmanship, tradition, and history that make each dram of whisky a memorable experience. Whether you're a seasoned enthusiast or a curious newcomer, a whisky distillery tour promises an intimate and enlightening adventure that will forever deepen your appreciation for this beloved spirit.

5.4 Eilean Donan Castle: Iconic Romance

Eilean Donan Castle, a quintessential Scottish landmark, embodies both history and romance in a breathtaking setting. Nestled on a small tidal island where three lochs — Loch Duich, Loch Long, and Loch Alsh — meet, the castle is a picturesque marvel that has captured the hearts of travelers for generations.

Dating back to the 13th century, Eilean Donan Castle has a rich history steeped in both war and peace. Originally built as a defensive stronghold to protect against Viking raids, the castle saw its fair share of battles and sieges over the centuries. It wasn't until the early 20th century that the dilapidated ruins were lovingly restored by Lt. Colonel John MacRae-Gilstrap. The restoration process carefully blended historic accuracy with modern amenities, preserving the castle's authenticity while making it accessible to visitors.

The castle's allure isn't solely tied to its history; it's also steeped in romance and legend. The name "Eilean Donan" translates to "Island of Donan," derived from the Irish saint Bishop Donan who established a Christian church on the island around the 6th century. This historical connection adds an element of mystique and spirituality to the castle's aura.

The setting itself is an embodiment of romantic imagery. Surrounded by sparkling waters, with the majestic mountains of the Scottish Highlands as a backdrop, Eilean Donan Castle stands as a testament to nature's beauty and human craftsmanship. As the sun sets over the lochs, casting a warm glow on the castle's stone walls, it's easy to see why this location has been a favorite for weddings, proposals, and even film shoots.

Indeed, Eilean Donan Castle's fame has transcended its historical significance. It gained international recognition when it appeared in several films, most notably in the 1986 movie "Highlander." This exposure further solidified its position as an iconic representation of Scotland's rugged beauty and timeless romance.

Visiting Eilean Donan Castle is an unforgettable experience. The castle's interior has been meticulously decorated to reflect different eras, offering visitors a glimpse into the past. The gift shop provides a variety of souvenirs, including Scottish crafts and tartans, allowing you to take a piece of the castle's charm home with you.

Whether you're a history enthusiast, a lover of scenic landscapes, or someone seeking a romantic escape, Eilean Donan Castle offers a journey through time and emotions. As you explore its towers, turrets, and courtyards, you can't help but be enchanted by the echoes of the past and the ever-present sense of romance that fills the air. A visit to this iconic Scottish landmark is an opportunity to connect with the heart of Scotland's history and experience a true tale of love, both in the stories that shaped it and the beauty that defines it.

5.5 Stargazing in Galloway Forest Park: Celestial Bonding

Galloway Forest Park, located in southwest Scotland, is a celestial haven for stargazers and astronomy enthusiasts. Renowned for its pristine skies and minimal light pollution, this park offers a unique opportunity to forge a celestial connection and delve into the mysteries of the universe.

Designated as the first Dark Sky Park in the UK and one of only a few Gold Tier Dark Sky Parks in the world by the International Dark-Sky Association, Galloway Forest Park boasts some of the darkest and clearest skies in Europe. This distinction is a testament to the efforts put forth to preserve the natural beauty of the night sky, allowing visitors to experience the wonders of astronomy without the interference of urban light pollution.

As the sun sets over Galloway Forest Park, the landscape transforms into a canvas of twinkling stars, planets, and galaxies. The Milky Way, that luminous band of countless stars stretching across the night sky, becomes a prominent feature, casting a sense of awe and wonder. With the naked eye, one can observe constellations and celestial objects that are often obscured in more populated areas.

For those seeking a more immersive experience, the park offers a variety of stargazing events and facilities. The Scottish Dark Sky Observatory, situated within the park, provides telescopes and knowledgeable guides to help visitors navigate the night sky. Guided tours, talks, and workshops offer a deeper understanding of astronomical phenomena, ensuring that both beginners and experienced stargazers can appreciate the wonders above.

To truly bond with the cosmos, consider bringing your own telescope or binoculars. Find a cozy spot along the tranquil shores of Loch Trool or in the heart of the forest, and let the vastness of space envelop you. The sheer magnitude of the universe becomes tangible as distant stars and galaxies come into view, bridging the gap between Earth and the cosmos.

Stargazing in Galloway Forest Park isn't limited to a single season; the park's dark skies are a year-round phenomenon. Each season offers its own unique celestial spectacles. From meteor showers that streak across the sky in the summer to the vivid constellations of winter, every visit promises a different celestial experience.

Before embarking on your stargazing adventure, it's essential to come prepared. Dress warmly, as even in the summer, nighttime temperatures can drop significantly. Bring a red flashlight to preserve your night vision, as white light can disrupt your ability to see faint celestial objects. And, of course, pack a star chart or a stargazing app to help you identify constellations and planets.

Stargazing in Galloway Forest Park is more than just an activity; it's an opportunity to bond with the universe, to contemplate our place in the cosmos, and to reconnect with the natural world. The park's dedication to preserving the beauty of the night sky ensures that every visit is a chance to experience the magic of the stars and planets, and to create memories that will last a lifetime. Whether you're a seasoned astronomer or simply curious about the universe, Galloway Forest Park invites you to look up and be captivated by the beauty that exists beyond our atmosphere.

5.6 Romantic Dinner Spots: Gastronomic Delights

Scotland, a land of stunning landscapes and rich history, offers an array of romantic dinner spots that combine gastronomic delights with breathtaking views. Whether you're celebrating an anniversary, a honeymoon, or simply looking to share an intimate meal, these enchanting venues provide the perfect backdrop for a memorable culinary experience.

1. The Witchery by the Castle, Edinburgh:

Nestled in the heart of Edinburgh, this historic restaurant exudes old-world charm. Set within a 16th-century building just steps away from the iconic Edinburgh Castle, Thc Witchery offers a gothic and luxurious atmosphere. Velvet drapes, candlelit tables, and ornate decor create a sense of opulence, while the menu showcases Scotland's finest ingredients. Indulge in dishes like haggis, Scottish venison, and locally-sourced seafood while immersing yourself in the romantic ambiance.

2. The Boath House, Nairn:
Surrounded by idyllic countryside, The Boath House is a boutique hotel with a Michelin-starred restaurant. The dining room overlooks the hotel's lush gardens, providing a serene and picturesque setting. The menu features seasonal ingredients, many of which are sourced from the property's own garden. Dine on inventive dishes crafted with precision and flair, all while enjoying the tranquility of the Scottish Highlands.

3. Rocpool Restaurant, Inverness:
Situated on the banks of the River Ness, Rocpool Restaurant offers a blend of modern sophistication and natural beauty. Floor-to-ceiling windows offer stunning views of the river and the city's charming Victorian architecture. The menu is a fusion of

contemporary and classic Scottish cuisine, and the restaurant's extensive wine list complements the dishes perfectly. With its urban elegance and riverfront setting, Rocpool creates an intimate and romantic ambiance.

4. Achnagairn Castle, Inverness:

For a touch of fairytale charm, Achnagairn Castle provides a remarkable dining experience. The castle's opulent dining room, complete with chandeliers and intricate woodwork, transports you to another era. With a focus on locally-sourced produce, the chefs create dishes that are both exquisite and flavorful. The castle's grandeur and the beauty of the surrounding grounds make it a splendid location for a romantic dinner.

5. Kinloch Lodge, Isle of Skye:

Perched on the rugged coastline of the Isle of Skye, Kinloch Lodge boasts not only breathtaking views of the sea but also a reputation for outstanding cuisine. The restaurant, situated within a historic family home, offers an intimate and cozy atmosphere. Indulge in a selection of traditional Scottish dishes with a modern twist, often featuring ingredients sourced from the island itself. As you dine, watch the sun dip below the horizon, casting a warm glow over the sea.

6. Café St Honoré, Edinburgh:
For a more relaxed yet equally romantic dining experience, Café St Honoré in Edinburgh offers a charming bistro atmosphere. With its commitment to sustainability and seasonal ingredients, the restaurant provides an ever-changing menu that reflects Scotland's culinary heritage. The cozy ambiance, soft lighting, and French-inspired decor create an inviting space for couples to enjoy an intimate meal.

From historic castles to waterfront views, Scotland's romantic dinner spots offer a diverse range of settings to celebrate love and savor the country's culinary treasures. Each venue not only provides exceptional gastronomy but also the opportunity to immerse yourself in Scotland's rich history, natural beauty, and the warmth of its hospitality. Whether you're indulging in a candlelit dinner within ancient walls or relishing local delicacies while surrounded by breathtaking landscapes, these dining experiences promise to create lasting memories for you and your loved one.

5.7 Secret Gardens and Hidden Gems: Intimate Discoveries

Scotland's charm extends beyond its well-known landmarks, offering a world of secret gardens and hidden gems that provide intimate and enchanting discoveries for travelers. These tucked-away treasures unveil a different side of Scotland, where nature, history, and serenity converge in unexpected places.

1. Glenwhan Gardens, Dumfries and Galloway:

Nestled on the rugged coastline of southwest Scotland, Glenwhan Gardens is a haven of tranquility and beauty. This hidden gem features a series of themed gardens, each with its own unique character. Wander through vibrant flower beds, meander along serene ponds, and admire panoramic views of the Irish Sea and Luce Bay. The sense of seclusion makes Glenwhan Gardens an ideal spot for quiet contemplation and leisurely strolls.

2. Drummond Castle Gardens, Perthshire:

Located near the charming town of Crieff, Drummond Castle Gardens is a carefully crafted masterpiece that has been featured in movies and TV series. The Italian-style terraced gardens boast immaculately maintained lawns, intricate parterres, and vibrant floral displays. These gardens, set against the backdrop of the majestic Drummond Castle, offer a sense of elegance and seclusion that transports visitors to another era.

3. Gairloch Garden, Wester Ross:
In the remote wilderness of the Scottish Highlands, Gairloch Garden presents a hidden paradise for nature enthusiasts. This private garden is a testament to the owners' dedication to preserving native plant species and fostering biodiversity. Meandering pathways lead you through woodlands, rock gardens, and water features, showcasing the rugged beauty of the Highlands and offering a glimpse of Scotland's untamed landscapes.

4. Inverewe Garden, Wester Ross:
Set against the dramatic backdrop of Loch Ewe, Inverewe Garden is a horticultural marvel that defies its remote location. Created in the 19th century, this lush oasis features exotic plants from around the world, thriving in a microclimate influenced by the Gulf Stream. Wandering through Inverewe's verdant landscapes is like stepping into a hidden paradise, with unexpected bursts of color and fragrance awaiting around every corner.

5. Little Sparta, Lanarkshire:

More than just a garden, Little Sparta is a work of art in itself. Created by the late artist and poet Ian Hamilton Finlay, this garden is a poetic landscape filled with sculptures, inscriptions, and installations that merge nature and language. Hidden within the Pentland Hills, Little Sparta invites visitors to explore its intricacies and engage in a thought-provoking dialogue between art, philosophy, and the natural world.

6. The Pineapple, Stirlingshire:

A true hidden gem, the Pineapple is an architectural oddity that sits amidst the Scottish countryside. This 18th-century folly was built as a summerhouse and symbol of wealth, featuring a pineapple-shaped dome on top. While not a traditional garden, the Pineapple's whimsical design and serene surroundings make it a unique spot for a leisurely picnic and a quirky photo opportunity.

These secret gardens and hidden gems offer a glimpse into Scotland's quieter, more intimate side. Away from the crowds, you can immerse yourself in nature's beauty, explore the legacy of artistic visionaries, and stumble upon unexpected treasures that reveal the country's rich tapestry of history and creativity. Whether you're seeking solace, inspiration, or simply a moment of wonder, these hidden corners of Scotland promise to provide an unforgettable and personal experience.

CHAPTER 6. Scottish Cuisine and Dining Experiences

6.1 Traditional Scottish Dishes to Try

Scotland is renowned for its rich culinary heritage, offering a variety of traditional dishes that are a must-try for any traveler. As you explore this picturesque country, be sure to indulge in these flavorful offerings that capture the essence of Scottish cuisine:

1. Haggis: One of the most iconic Scottish dishes, haggis is a savory pudding made from sheep's offal (heart, liver, and lungs), combined with suet, oatmeal, onions, and spices. It's traditionally encased in a sheep's stomach lining and then boiled. Haggis is often served with "neeps and tatties" (mashed turnips and potatoes) and a whisky sauce. Don't be put off by its ingredients; the combination results in a hearty and surprisingly delicious dish.

2. Cullen Skink: A hearty Scottish soup, Cullen Skink features smoked haddock, potatoes, onions, and milk or cream. It has a creamy texture and is flavored with parsley and sometimes leeks. This comforting soup is a perfect choice, especially during the colder months.

3. Scotch Pie: This handheld meat pie is a favorite snack in Scotland. It typically contains minced meat (often beef or mutton), seasoned with spices, and encased in a crisp, golden-brown pastry crust. Enjoy it as a quick bite on the go.

4. Cock-a-Leekie Soup: A traditional Scottish soup made from chicken, leeks, and prunes, Cock-a-Leekie Soup is a delightful blend of sweet and savory flavors. It's a dish that showcases the harmonious use of local ingredients.

5. Porridge: A staple breakfast dish, Scottish porridge is made from oats simmered in water or milk until it reaches a thick, creamy consistency. It's often served with a drizzle of honey, cream, or a sprinkle of brown sugar. Porridge is not only nutritious but also an authentic way to start your day.

6. Black Pudding: Also known as "blood pudding," this sausage-like dish is made from a mixture of pork blood, fat, oats, and spices. It's then sliced and fried or grilled until crispy on the outside. Black pudding is a unique addition to a traditional Scottish breakfast.

7. Clootie Dumpling: A dessert that dates back centuries, clootie dumpling is a spiced pudding made with flour, breadcrumbs, suet, sugar, currants, and spices. It's traditionally boiled in a cloth (clootie) and served with custard or cream.

8. Salmon: Scotland is famous for its high-quality salmon, both farmed and wild-caught. Whether it's smoked, grilled, or cured, Scottish salmon is a culinary delight that offers a taste of the country's pristine waters.

9. Shortbread: A buttery and crumbly biscuit, shortbread is a beloved Scottish treat. Made from simple ingredients like butter, sugar, and flour, it comes in various shapes and sizes. Shortbread is often enjoyed with a cup of tea or coffee.

10. Dundee Cake: This fruitcake hailing from the city of Dundee is made with almonds, currants, sultanas, and candied peel. It's characterized by its distinctive almond topping and is often enjoyed during holidays and special occasions.

Exploring these traditional Scottish dishes is a delightful way to immerse yourself in the country's culture and history. From hearty meals to sweet treats, each dish tells a story of Scotland's culinary evolution over the centuries. Remember to pair your meals with a sip of Scotch whisky to complete your gastronomic journey!

6.2 Top Restaurants for Families

Scotland offers a plethora of family-friendly restaurants that cater to a diverse range of tastes and preferences. Here are some top choices to consider while planning your family trip:

1. The Witchery by the Castle, Edinburgh: Located near the iconic Edinburgh Castle, this restaurant offers a magical dining experience for families. The historic and charming atmosphere combined with a children's menu ensures a memorable meal for all ages.

2. Brel, Glasgow: With a beautiful garden setting, Brel in Glasgow provides a relaxed and family-friendly atmosphere. The menu features a variety of dishes, including options for children, making it an ideal spot for a casual family lunch or dinner.

3. Café St Honore, Edinburgh: This restaurant prides itself on using locally-sourced ingredients to create delicious French and Scottish fusion dishes.

The warm and welcoming ambiance is perfect for families seeking a cozy dining experience.

4. The Dome, Edinburgh: If you're looking for an elegant yet family-friendly restaurant, The Dome is a great choice. The stunning interior and diverse menu, which includes options for kids, make it a wonderful place to enjoy a special meal together.

5. Ubiquitous Chip, Glasgow: Known for its artistic and quirky decor, Ubiquitous Chip offers a unique dining experience for families. The outdoor terrace is particularly popular during warmer months, providing a pleasant space for families to enjoy their meal.

6. The Peat Inn, St Andrews: If you're exploring the St Andrews area, The Peat Inn is worth a visit. With a Michelin-starred restaurant and a more casual pub setting, it offers options to suit different preferences and occasions.

7. Mimi's Bakehouse, Edinburgh: Families with a sweet tooth will adore Mimi's Bakehouse. Famous for its delectable cakes, pastries, and afternoon teas, this spot is perfect for a delightful treat with your loved ones.

8. Ox and Finch, Glasgow: Offering a contemporary and shared-dining concept, Ox and Finch provides an interactive dining experience that can be enjoyed by families. The menu is designed for sharing, allowing everyone to sample a variety of dishes.

9. Maison Bleue, Edinburgh: This restaurant blends Scottish, French, and North African cuisines to create a unique fusion of flavors. The diverse menu and welcoming ambiance make it suitable for families seeking something a bit different.

10. Pizza Express, Various Locations: If you're looking for a reliable option that kids are sure to enjoy, Pizza Express has multiple locations across Scotland. Their family-friendly atmosphere, customizable pizzas, and activities for children make it a hit with families.

Remember that it's always a good idea to make reservations in advance, especially if you're visiting during peak tourist seasons. Additionally, some restaurants might have specific family-oriented events or promotions, so be sure to check their websites or call ahead for more information. Enjoy your culinary adventures with your family in Scotland!

6.3 Romantic Dining Spots for Couples

Certainly, Scotland offers a range of enchanting dining spots that are perfect for couples seeking a romantic culinary experience. Whether you're looking for a candlelit dinner overlooking stunning landscapes or an intimate setting with exquisite cuisine, Scotland has something to offer every romantic palate. Here are some top choices for couples looking to create unforgettable memories:

1. The Witchery by the Castle, Edinburgh: Nestled near the iconic Edinburgh Castle, The Witchery offers an opulent and romantic atmosphere. With its gothic charm, candlelit tables, and rich decor, this restaurant sets the stage for an enchanting evening. The indulgent menu and extensive wine list complement the romantic ambiance.

2. The Tower Restaurant, Edinburgh: Situated atop the National Museum of Scotland, The Tower Restaurant boasts panoramic views of the city's skyline. Its elegant setting, contemporary Scottish cuisine, and a diverse selection of wines create a sophisticated dining experience for couples.

3. Rocpool Reserve, Inverness: This boutique hotel and restaurant offers a luxurious dining experience in Inverness. The stylish decor, attentive service,

and modern Scottish dishes make it an ideal choice for couples celebrating a special occasion.

4. The Peat Inn, St Andrews: A Michelin-starred restaurant with a romantic country inn setting, The Peat Inn provides an intimate and cozy atmosphere. Couples can enjoy a fine dining experience with seasonal ingredients and exceptional wine pairings.

5. Boath House, Nairn: Set within a charming Georgian mansion, Boath House offers a romantic escape in the Highlands. The restaurant's exquisite cuisine, featuring locally-sourced ingredients, is served in an elegant dining room with views of the surrounding gardens.

6. The Albannach, Lochinver: If you're exploring the stunning landscapes of the Scottish Highlands, The Albannach provides a unique dining experience. With its remote location and focus on fresh seafood and local produce, couples can savor each other's company while enjoying authentic Scottish flavors.

7. The Ubiquitous Chip, Glasgow: With its whimsical decor and romantic garden terrace, The Ubiquitous Chip is a popular choice for couples seeking an artistic and atmospheric setting. The

creative menu and extensive wine selection add to the allure.

8. Aizle, Edinburgh: Aizle offers a contemporary and innovative dining experience. The tasting menu, which features ever-changing seasonal ingredients, creates an element of surprise that can make your romantic dinner truly memorable.

9. Kinloch Lodge, Isle of Skye: Located on the breathtaking Isle of Skye, Kinloch Lodge combines exceptional dining with breathtaking views. Couples can savor refined Scottish cuisine while taking in the natural beauty of the island.

10. The Kitchin, Edinburgh: Helmed by Michelin-starred chef Tom Kitchin, this restaurant offers a blend of French techniques and Scottish ingredients. Its cozy and inviting atmosphere, along with the use of local produce, sets the stage for a memorable romantic meal.

Remember to make reservations in advance, as these romantic dining spots can fill up quickly, especially during peak tourist seasons. Each of these restaurants offers a unique experience that captures the essence of Scotland's romantic charm, making them perfect for couples looking to celebrate their love in a truly special way.

6.4 Vegetarian and Vegan-Friendly Options

Scotland has embraced the growing trend of vegetarian and vegan cuisine, offering a wide range of options for those seeking plant-based dining experiences. From bustling cities to quaint towns, you'll find restaurants, cafes, and eateries that cater to vegetarian and vegan preferences. Here's an extensive guide to help you navigate through Scotland's vegetarian and vegan-friendly culinary scene:

Edinburgh:
1. Henderson's: A beloved institution, Henderson's offers a variety of vegan and vegetarian dishes made with locally sourced ingredients. Their salad bar and daily specials are a hit among diners.
2. David Bann: This upscale vegetarian restaurant offers a diverse menu featuring creative and flavorful dishes, from hearty mains to exquisite desserts.
3. Novapizza Vegetarian Kitchen: If you're a pizza lover, Novapizza is a must-visit. They specialize in gourmet vegetarian and vegan pizzas with a variety of innovative toppings.

Glasgow:
1. Mono: A vegan bar and restaurant, Mono not only offers delicious plant-based food but also hosts live music events and a record store, creating a vibrant and unique atmosphere.
2. The 78 Bar and Kitchen: With a diverse menu featuring comfort food favorites and global cuisine, The 78 is a popular spot for vegans and vegetarians in Glasgow.
3. Saramago Café Bar: Located within the Centre for Contemporary Arts, Saramago offers a selection of vegan and vegetarian dishes in an artistic and cultural setting.

Aberdeen:
1. Foodstory Café: This eco-friendly café is committed to serving organic, vegan, and gluten-free options. It's a cozy spot for enjoying healthy meals, smoothies, and baked goods.
2. Bonobo Café: With a fully vegan menu, Bonobo Café offers a range of dishes from burgers to salads, all made from scratch using fresh ingredients.

Dundee:
1. Marwick's Vegan Kitchen: A family-run establishment, Marwick's offers an array of vegan

comfort foods, including burgers, wraps, and delectable desserts.

2. Forge: A vegan café that focuses on nourishing and wholesome food, Forge serves everything from hearty breakfasts to creative lunch options.

Isle of Skye:
1. Skye Pie Café: This charming café offers savory and sweet pies, with vegetarian and vegan options available. It's a perfect stop for a warm and satisfying meal.

Inverness:
1. The Kitchen: A vegan and vegetarian-friendly eatery, The Kitchen serves a mix of international and locally inspired dishes, with a focus on fresh, seasonal ingredients.

Stirling:
1. Nana's: A vegan café known for its friendly atmosphere, Nana's serves an array of homemade dishes, cakes, and treats.

Tips for Exploring Vegetarian and Vegan Options:
- Look for menu symbols or indications that highlight vegetarian and vegan dishes.

- Don't hesitate to ask for modifications or substitutions to make dishes vegan-friendly.
- Check online reviews or use food-focused apps to discover more hidden gems and recommendations.
- Be open to trying traditional Scottish dishes that have been creatively adapted to be vegetarian or vegan.

Scotland's culinary scene has evolved to accommodate diverse dietary preferences, making it an exciting destination for vegetarians and vegans. From hearty meals to delicate desserts, you'll find a variety of flavors that cater to plant-based palates, allowing you to savor the best of Scottish cuisine while enjoying ethical and sustainable dining.

6.5 Whisky Tasting and Distillery Experiences

Scotland is renowned for its rich whisky heritage, offering visitors a chance to immerse themselves in the world of whisky tasting and distillery experiences. From the picturesque landscapes of the Highlands to the historic cities, here's an extensive guide to help you navigate through Scotland's whisky culture:

Types of Scotch Whisky:

1. Single Malt: Made from malted barley and produced at a single distillery, single malt whiskies are known for their diverse flavors and distinct characteristics.

2. Blended Scotch: A blend of different malt and grain whiskies from multiple distilleries, blended Scotch whiskies offer a balanced and consistent taste profile.

3. Single Grain: Produced using grains other than malted barley, single grain whiskies can offer a lighter and sweeter flavor profile.

4. Blended Malt: Formerly known as "vatted malts," blended malt whiskies combine single malts from different distilleries, allowing for a range of flavors.

Distillery Experiences:
1. The Scotch Whisky Experience, Edinburgh: This interactive attraction takes visitors through the whisky-making process, complete with a barrel ride and a vast collection of whiskies.

2. Glenfiddich Distillery, Dufftown: A pioneer in single malt Scotch, Glenfiddich offers guided tours showcasing its traditional distilling methods and a chance to explore their extensive whisky collection.

3. Laphroaig Distillery, Islay: For those who love peaty whiskies, Laphroaig on the Isle of Islay provides a unique opportunity to experience the distinctive smoky flavors of their single malts.

4. The Macallan Distillery, Craigellachie: Known for its exceptional quality, The Macallan offers a modern distillery experience and an impressive range of premium whiskies.

5. Talisker Distillery, Isle of Skye: Located on the rugged Isle of Skye, Talisker offers tours that delve into their maritime influence and the distinct flavors it imparts.

6. Glenlivet Distillery, Ballindalloch: As one of the oldest legal distilleries in Scotland, Glenlivet offers insights into the history of whisky production and a variety of guided tours.

Whisky Tasting:
1. Whisky Bars: Cities like Edinburgh and Glasgow boast an array of whisky bars where you can sample a wide selection of Scotch whiskies from different regions and distilleries.

2. Whisky Festivals: Scotland hosts numerous whisky festivals throughout the year, providing opportunities to taste rare and limited-edition releases, attend masterclasses, and engage with industry experts.

3. Tasting Events at Distilleries: Many distilleries offer guided tastings as part of their tours, allowing you to explore various expressions and learn about tasting techniques.

Tips for Enjoying Whisky Tasting:
- Start with the Basics: If you're new to whisky, begin with milder options and gradually explore more complex flavors.
- Use Your Senses: Observe the color, inhale the aroma, and savor the taste. Whisky tasting is a multisensory experience.
- Experiment with Water: A few drops of water can open up the flavors and aromas of whisky, so don't hesitate to add a little and see how it changes.

Scotland's whisky scene offers an unforgettable journey into its history, craftsmanship, and diverse range of flavors. Whether you're a connoisseur or a novice, exploring distilleries and tasting different types of Scotch whiskies is an essential part of experiencing the country's rich cultural tapestry.

6.6 Best Places for Afternoon Tea

Indulging in afternoon tea is a quintessential British tradition, and Scotland offers a delightful array of venues where you can savor this experience. From charming tearooms to elegant hotels, here's an extensive guide to the best places for afternoon tea in Scotland:

Edinburgh:

1. The Balmoral: This iconic hotel offers a luxurious afternoon tea experience in its Palm Court, featuring an assortment of sandwiches, scones, pastries, and a wide selection of teas.

2. Palm Court at The Principal Edinburgh George Street: With its stunning glass dome and opulent decor, Palm Court offers a sumptuous afternoon tea featuring both classic and contemporary treats.

3. Eteaket: A modern tea room known for its creative tea blends, Eteaket offers afternoon tea with a twist, including both traditional and vegan options.

Glasgow:

1. Blythswood Square Hotel: Enjoy a sophisticated afternoon tea experience at this 5-star hotel,

complete with an array of finger sandwiches, scones, cakes, and fine teas.

2. The Willow Tea Rooms: Designed by Charles Rennie Mackintosh, this tearoom offers a blend of art, history, and delectable treats. Choose from a variety of afternoon tea options.

3. The Cup and Saucer Tearoom: A charming tearoom with a vintage vibe, The Cup and Saucer offers a delightful afternoon tea featuring homemade scones, cakes, and sandwiches.

Perthshire:
1. Gleneagles: This luxury resort offers a lavish afternoon tea experience with a variety of delicacies served in a picturesque setting.

2. Fonab Castle Hotel & Spa: Enjoy a traditional afternoon tea while taking in panoramic views of Loch Faskally and the surrounding mountains.

St. Andrews:
1. Old Course Hotel: Overlooking the famous Old Course, this hotel offers an elegant afternoon tea experience with freshly baked scones, finger sandwiches, and pastries.

Aberdeen:
1. The Chester Hotel: Known for its contemporary twist on afternoon tea, The Chester Hotel offers a delightful selection of sweet and savory treats.

Isle of Skye:
1. Kinloch Lodge: With stunning views of the Isle of Skye's landscapes, Kinloch Lodge provides a memorable afternoon tea experience with homemade pastries and cakes.

Scottish Borders:
1. Cringletie House Hotel: This charming country house hotel offers a traditional afternoon tea experience in a tranquil setting.

Highlands:
1. The Torridon: Nestled in the Highlands, The Torridon offers a unique twist on afternoon tea, featuring locally sourced ingredients and stunning views.

Tips for Enjoying Afternoon Tea:
- Reservations: Many venues require reservations, especially during peak hours and tourist seasons, so it's wise to book in advance.

- Dress Code: Some high-end establishments might have a dress code, so it's a good idea to inquire beforehand.
- Dietary Restrictions: Inform the venue in advance if you have any dietary restrictions or preferences to ensure they can accommodate your needs.
- Take Your Time: Afternoon tea is meant to be a leisurely affair, so take your time to enjoy each course and the company of your companions.

Indulging in afternoon tea in Scotland allows you to experience not only delicious food and exquisite teas but also the country's warm hospitality and charming ambience. Whether you're in a bustling city or a serene countryside, these venues offer an opportunity to create cherished memories and relish in a time-honored tradition.

6.7 Unique Food Markets and Street Food Delights

Scotland's food markets and street food scene offer a diverse and flavorful culinary experience that reflects the country's rich heritage and modern innovation. From bustling city markets to charming coastal towns, here's an extensive guide to the unique food markets and street food delights in Scotland:

Glasgow:

1. Buchanan Street Food Market: Located in the heart of the city, this market features a variety of street food vendors offering global cuisine, from gourmet burgers to Asian fusion dishes.

2. Big Feed: This indoor street food market is a weekend hotspot, bringing together a wide range of vendors offering everything from tacos to vegan treats.

3. Platform at the Argyle Street Arches: Housed in a historic archway, this street food market offers an eclectic mix of cuisines, craft beer, and live music events.

Edinburgh:

1. Edinburgh Farmers' Market: Held every Saturday, this market showcases local produce, artisanal cheeses, fresh seafood, and more, allowing you to taste the best of Scottish ingredients.

2. The Pitt: A vibrant street food market that hosts a rotating lineup of food stalls, craft beer, and live music in a hip and industrial setting.

3. Stockbridge Market: Offering a mix of food, crafts, and vintage goods, this market is a delightful place to sample artisanal treats and local products.

Aberdeen:

1. The Aberdeen Market: This indoor market is a food lover's paradise, featuring a wide variety of stalls offering fresh produce, meats, and international foods.

Dundee:

1. The Food Life: A popular street food event that gathers local vendors and food trucks, offering a diverse range of cuisines and flavors.

Stirling:

1. Stirling Farmers' Market: Held on the second Saturday of each month, this market showcases fresh local produce, artisanal goods, and delectable treats.

Perth:

1. Perth Farmers' Market: This market features over 50 stalls offering everything from traditional Scottish fare to international delights, along with live music and entertainment.

Isle of Skye:

1. Skye Farmers' Market: Held on the first Saturday of the month, this market highlights Skye's local produce, seafood, and crafts, allowing visitors to sample the island's flavors.

Tips for Exploring Food Markets and Street Food:
- Arrive Hungry: Come with an empty stomach so you can enjoy a variety of flavors and dishes.
- Cash and Cards: While many vendors accept cards, it's a good idea to carry some cash for smaller transactions.
- Ask Questions: Don't hesitate to ask vendors about their dishes and ingredients; they often love to share their passion for food.
- Try Something New: Use this opportunity to try dishes you may not have experienced before, embracing local and global flavors.

Scotland's food markets and street food scene offer a unique blend of traditional and contemporary flavors, providing a window into the country's culinary diversity. Whether you're strolling through a bustling urban market or savoring street food by the seaside, you'll discover a world of tastes that reflect Scotland's vibrant culture and gastronomic innovation.

CHAPTER 7. Outdoor Adventures and Activities

7.1 Hiking Trails for All Skill Levels

Scotland's stunning landscapes are a paradise for outdoor enthusiasts, offering hiking trails that cater to all skill levels. From leisurely walks to challenging climbs, here's an extensive guide to some of the best hiking trails in Scotland for every type of hiker:

Easy Trails:

1. Arthur's Seat, Edinburgh: A relatively short hike within the city, Arthur's Seat offers panoramic views of Edinburgh and the surrounding countryside.

2. Fairy Pools, Isle of Skye: A gentle walk through picturesque glens leads to these magical pools and waterfalls, perfect for a relaxing day out.

3. Loch an Eilein, Cairngorms National Park: This tranquil walk takes you around a beautiful loch with a 13th-century castle on an island.

Moderate Trails:

1. Ben A'an, Trossachs National Park: A rewarding climb with breathtaking views over Loch Katrine, suitable for those looking for a moderate challenge.

2. Glen Nevis, Fort William: The hike through Glen Nevis offers views of the UK's highest peak, Ben Nevis, and takes you through scenic valleys and woods.

3. Conic Hill, Loch Lomond and The Trossachs: A popular hike with stunning views of Loch Lomond and surrounding mountains, accessible from the charming village of Balmaha.

Challenging Trails:

1. Buachaille Etive Mòr, Glencoe: Known as the "Great Herdsman of Etive," this iconic mountain offers a challenging ascent and panoramic views of Glencoe.

2. The Cobbler (Ben Arthur), Arrochar: This hike offers a mixture of rocky paths and scrambling, leading to stunning vistas of Loch Long and the surrounding mountains.

3. Cairn Gorm, Cairngorms National Park: A strenuous climb, Cairn Gorm rewards hikers with

incredible views from its summit and the opportunity to explore Scotland's alpine flora.

Long-Distance Trails:

1. West Highland Way: One of Scotland's most famous long-distance trails, this 96-mile route takes you through diverse landscapes, from Lowland moors to Highland mountains.

2. Great Glen Way: This 79-mile trail follows the natural fault line of the Great Glen, connecting Fort William to Inverness along the Caledonian Canal.

3. Southern Upland Way: Stretching coast-to-coast across Scotland, this challenging trail offers diverse landscapes and breathtaking views.

Coastal Trails:

1. Fife Coastal Path: Running along the picturesque coastline, this trail offers stunning sea views, historic sites, and charming fishing villages.

2. Kintyre Way: This trail follows the Kintyre Peninsula's coastline, providing walkers with stunning vistas of islands, beaches, and cliffs.

Tips for Hiking in Scotland:
- Weather Preparedness: Scotland's weather can be unpredictable, so always carry waterproof clothing, warm layers, and suitable footwear.
- Navigation: Familiarize yourself with the trail and carry a map, compass, or GPS device, especially for more remote routes.
- Wildlife Awareness: Respect the natural environment and wildlife. Be aware of seasonal nesting sites and follow "Leave No Trace" principles.
- Emergency Contact: Inform someone of your hiking plans and estimated return time, especially for more challenging trails.

Scotland's hiking trails offer a diverse range of experiences, from tranquil strolls through scenic landscapes to challenging climbs with breathtaking vistas. Whether you're a beginner or an experienced hiker, you'll find a trail that suits your skill level and provides an opportunity to immerse yourself in the country's rugged beauty and outdoor adventure.

7.2 Cycling Routes and Bike Rentals

Scotland's diverse landscapes, from rugged mountains to serene lochs, provide an incredible backdrop for cyclists of all levels. Whether you're a leisurely rider or a dedicated enthusiast, Scotland offers a wide range of cycling routes and bike rental options to explore its natural beauty. Here's an extensive guide to cycling routes and bike rentals in Scotland:

Cycling Routes:

1. The North Coast 500 (NC500): This iconic 516-mile circular route takes you around the stunning Highlands, passing through picturesque villages, historic sites, and breathtaking coastal scenery.

2. Lochs and Glens Cycle Route: Stretching from Glasgow to Inverness, this 215-mile route takes you through charming lochs, glens, and forests, providing a tranquil cycling experience.

3. Great Glen Cycle Route: Running alongside the Caledonian Canal, this 79-mile route connects Fort William to Inverness, offering a mix of scenic landscapes and historic landmarks.

4. Hebridean Way Cycling Route: Explore the Outer Hebrides along this 185-mile route, passing through a chain of islands with stunning beaches, rugged cliffs, and Gaelic culture.

5. Tweed Cycleway: Following the River Tweed from Biggar to Berwick-upon-Tweed, this route offers a mix of historic towns, countryside, and riverside paths.

6. Five Ferries Cycle Route: Combining cycling with ferry crossings, this circular route takes you through the picturesque landscapes of the Clyde and the stunning Kintyre Peninsula.

Bike Rentals:

1. Bike Rental Shops: Many cities and towns in Scotland have bike rental shops that offer a variety of options, from hybrid bikes for leisurely rides to mountain bikes for more challenging terrain.

2. Cycle Hire Centers: Located near popular cycling routes, these centers offer a range of bikes suitable for different terrains, along with helmets, locks, and other essential gear.

3. E-Bike Rentals: Electric bikes (e-bikes) are becoming increasingly popular and can be rented from various locations, providing an extra boost for tackling hills and longer distances.

4. Guided Cycling Tours: If you prefer a guided experience, some rental shops offer guided cycling tours led by experienced local guides who can provide insights into the area's history and culture.

Tips for Cycling in Scotland:
- Weather Preparedness: Scotland's weather can change quickly, so dress in layers and carry waterproof clothing.
- Safety First: Always wear a helmet, especially on unfamiliar routes or challenging terrain.
- Road Etiquette: Observe traffic rules, use hand signals, and be courteous to other road users.
- Navigation: Carry a map, GPS device, or smartphone app to help you navigate the routes.
- Wildlife Awareness: When cycling through rural areas, be mindful of wildlife and follow local guidelines.

Scotland's cycling routes offer a fantastic way to explore its diverse landscapes, from the dramatic Highlands to the serene coastlines. Whether you're a leisure cyclist or a seasoned rider, the country's well-maintained routes and bike rental options provide endless opportunities for adventure and discovery. So, hop on a bike, pedal your way through Scotland, and experience its beauty up close!

7.3 Water Sports and Kayaking Opportunities

Scotland, with its breathtaking landscapes and pristine waters, offers a paradise for water sports enthusiasts and kayakers alike. From tranquil lochs to exhilarating rapids, Scotland's diverse aquatic playground provides endless opportunities for adventure and exploration. Whether you're a seasoned kayaker or a beginner looking to dip your paddle into the world of water sports, Scotland has something to offer for everyone.

1. Lochs and Lakes:

Scotland's numerous lochs and lakes are perfect for kayaking. Loch Ness, famed for its mysterious monster, is a must-visit destination. Paddle along its serene waters while taking in the stunning views of the surrounding Highlands. Loch Lomond, the largest freshwater loch in Great Britain, is another popular kayaking spot. Its islands, quiet coves, and clear waters provide a picturesque backdrop for your adventure.

2. Coastal Excursions:

The rugged Scottish coastline presents kayakers with a unique opportunity to explore sea caves, arches, and hidden beaches. The Argyll coast, with its sheltered bays and dramatic cliffs, is a prime location for coastal kayaking. Keep an eye out for seals, dolphins, and a variety of seabirds that often accompany kayakers on their journeys.

3. White Water Thrills:
For those seeking an adrenaline rush, Scotland's white-water rivers offer an exciting challenge. The River Spey and River Findhorn are renowned for their white-water rapids, catering to kayakers with varying skill levels. Join guided tours led by experienced instructors to navigate these exhilarating waters safely.

4. Canoe Trails:
Scotland boasts an array of canoe trails, providing a unique way to explore the country's waterways. The Great Glen Canoe Trail traverses the Caledonian Canal and takes you through the heart of the Highlands. The Spey Descent Canoe Trail offers a more leisurely paddle along the scenic River Spey, passing through lush landscapes and charming villages.

5. Equipment Rental and Tours:
No kayak? No problem. Scotland has a plethora of rental shops and tour operators that provide equipment and guided experiences. Whether you're a novice or an expert, these services cater to various

skill levels and preferences. Local guides not only ensure your safety but also share their knowledge of the area's history and natural wonders.

6. Safety and Environmental Considerations:

Before embarking on any water sports adventure, it's crucial to prioritize safety. Check weather conditions, wear appropriate gear, and inform someone about your plans. Scotland's weather can be unpredictable, so always be prepared for changes. Additionally, respect the environment by following the Leave No Trace principles, ensuring that these stunning natural spaces remain pristine for future generations.

Scotland's water sports and kayaking opportunities offer a gateway to explore the country's diverse aquatic landscapes. Whether you're seeking tranquility on a tranquil loch, thrills on white-water rapids, or coastal adventures along rugged cliffs, Scotland has it all. Embrace the unique experiences, immerse yourself in the breathtaking scenery, and create memories that will last a lifetime on the enchanting waters of Scotland.

7.4 Golfing in Scotland: Legendary Courses

Scotland is the birthplace of golf and holds a special place in the hearts of golf enthusiasts worldwide. The country's rich history, stunning landscapes, and iconic courses make it a pilgrimage destination for golfers seeking to experience the sport in its truest form. From ancient links courses to modern championship layouts, Scotland offers a golfing experience like no other.

1. St. Andrews - The Home of Golf:
No discussion about golf in Scotland is complete without mentioning St. Andrews. This historic town is often referred to as the "Home of Golf." The Old Course, with its iconic Swilcan Bridge and Hell Bunker, is one of the most revered and challenging courses in the world. St. Andrews Links comprises several other courses, including the New Course and the Jubilee Course, providing a variety of playing experiences for golfers of all skill levels.

2. Muirfield - A Timeless Classic:
Muirfield, located in East Lothian, is another legendary course that has hosted numerous Open Championships. Known for its demanding yet fair layout, Muirfield challenges golfers with its strategic bunkering and undulating fairways. The

course's design stands the test of time, providing a true test of golfing prowess.

3. Royal Troon - Championship Elegance:
Royal Troon, situated on the Ayrshire coast, boasts both a rich history and a challenging layout. The Old Course at Royal Troon features the famous "Postage Stamp" par-3 hole, known for its small green and challenging bunkers. With its dramatic coastline views and strong prevailing winds, Royal Troon is a must-play course for any golfer.

4. Carnoustie - A Golfer's Toughest Challenge:
Carnoustie Golf Links is renowned for being one of the toughest challenges in golf. Its Championship Course has hosted several Open Championships and is notorious for its unforgiving rough, deep bunkers, and unpredictable weather conditions. Carnoustie offers a true test of skill and mental fortitude, making it a favorite among serious golfers.

5. Turnberry - Awe-Inspiring Beauty:
Turnberry, part of the Trump Turnberry Resort, is set against the backdrop of the Ailsa Craig and the Irish Sea. The Ailsa Course is known for its breathtaking views, challenging holes, and rich

history of hosting major championships. The recent renovations have elevated Turnberry's status, making it a bucket-list course for golfers seeking a luxurious golfing experience.

6. Gleneagles - Luxury and Tradition:
Gleneagles, a luxury resort in Perthshire, is home to three championship courses: the King's Course, the Queen's Course, and the PGA Centenary Course. The latter hosted the 2014 Ryder Cup. Each course offers a unique golfing experience, combining challenging holes with stunning scenery.

Golfing in Scotland is an experience that transcends the sport itself. The country's legendary courses, steeped in history and surrounded by breathtaking landscapes, offer golfers the chance to walk in the footsteps of legends. From the timeless challenges of St. Andrews to the dramatic beauty of Turnberry, Scotland's golf courses provide a journey that every golfer should embark upon. Whether you're a professional seeking a test of skill or an amateur wanting to immerse yourself in the sport's heritage, Scotland's legendary courses are waiting to welcome you to their fairways.

7.5 Wildlife Watching and Bird Sanctuaries

Scotland's diverse and picturesque landscapes offer a haven for wildlife enthusiasts and birdwatchers alike. From rugged mountains to serene lochs, Scotland's natural beauty provides the perfect backdrop for observing a wide variety of wildlife species. Whether you're an avid birder or simply seeking a closer connection with nature, Scotland's abundant wildlife and well-preserved habitats promise an unforgettable experience.

1. Bird Sanctuaries and Reserves:

Scotland boasts a number of bird sanctuaries and reserves that are dedicated to the conservation and protection of avian species. RSPB (Royal Society for the Protection of Birds) reserves are spread throughout the country, providing opportunities to observe rare and iconic birds in their natural habitats. Notable sanctuaries include:

- Firth of Forth: Home to the famous Bass Rock, which hosts one of the world's largest colonies of gannets. The Isle of May is another key location for seabird colonies.

- Loch Leven: A haven for waterbirds, including whooper swans, pochards, and ospreys. The Loch

Leven Heritage Trail offers excellent bird watching opportunities.

 - Handa Island: A remote island off the northwest coast, known for its puffin colonies and dramatic cliffs. Accessible by boat, it offers a unique bird watching experience.

 - Caerlaverock Wetland Centre: A wintering ground for thousands of barnacle geese and other waterfowl. The center provides observation hides and guided tours.

2. Iconic Wildlife Species:
Scotland's diverse ecosystems support a range of wildlife species, both on land and in water. Keep an eye out for:

 - Red Deer: Scotland's largest land mammal, often spotted in the Highlands and Cairngorms National Park.

 - Golden Eagles: Majestic birds of prey that inhabit mountainous regions, such as the Cairngorms and the Isle of Skye.

- Red Squirrels: Found in woodland areas, these charming creatures are a delight to spot, especially in places like the Cairngorms and the Trossachs.

- Otters: Coastal areas and freshwater lochs are prime spots to catch a glimpse of these elusive and playful creatures.

- Seals: The Moray Firth and Orkney Islands are popular spots for observing seals in their natural habitat.

3. Wildlife Tours and Guides:
To make the most of your wildlife watching experience, consider joining guided tours led by knowledgeable experts. These guides can help you locate and identify various species while sharing insights into their behaviors and habitats. Whether you're exploring the rugged landscapes of the Highlands or the coastal wonders of the west coast, wildlife tours offer an immersive and educational adventure.

4. Responsible Wildlife Watching:
When observing wildlife, it's important to do so responsibly to ensure the safety and well-being of the animals and their habitats. Maintain a respectful distance, avoid disturbing nesting sites,

and follow the "Leave No Trace" principles to minimize your impact on the environment.

Scotland's rich biodiversity and pristine landscapes make it a paradise for wildlife enthusiasts and birdwatchers. From rare birds to iconic mammals, the country's diverse ecosystems offer endless opportunities for observation and appreciation. Whether you're exploring bird sanctuaries, embarking on wildlife tours, or simply taking a leisurely stroll through the countryside, Scotland's natural beauty and abundant wildlife will leave you with lasting memories of your unforgettable journey.

7.6 Rock Climbing and Abseiling Spots

Scotland's rugged terrain, dramatic cliffs, and towering mountains make it a paradise for rock climbers and abseilers seeking thrilling outdoor adventures. With a wide range of routes catering to various skill levels, Scotland offers opportunities for both beginners and experienced climbers to test their abilities against the elements. From the iconic sea stacks to the challenging crags, Scotland's rock climbing and abseiling spots promise exhilarating experiences and breathtaking vistas.

1. Ben Nevis - A Highland Challenge:

Ben Nevis, the UK's highest peak, offers a variety of rock climbing routes for enthusiasts of all levels. Tower Ridge is a classic route that involves both climbing and abseiling, providing panoramic views and an unforgettable mountaineering experience. The North Face of Ben Nevis presents challenging routes for experienced climbers, while the Carn Dearg Buttress is a popular choice for those seeking a more moderate climb.

2. Isle of Skye - Sea Stacks and Skye Ridge:

The Isle of Skye is a rock climber's paradise, offering a mix of sea stack climbing and mountain routes. The Old Man of Storr and the Quiraing are renowned for their unique geological formations and provide opportunities for both climbing and abseiling. The Cuillin Ridge is a major highlight, with a challenging traverse that requires mountaineering skills and offers spectacular views.

3. Glen Coe - Iconic Scottish Scenery:

Glen Coe is famous for its breathtaking scenery and offers a range of climbing and abseiling options. The Aonach Eagach Ridge is a thrilling traverse that tests climbers' skills and nerve, while Buachaille Etive Mor provides a variety of routes for climbers of different levels. The challenging routes amidst the backdrop of rugged peaks make Glen Coe a rock climbing haven.

4. Arrochar Alps - Thrills by Loch Long:
The Arrochar Alps, located by Loch Long, offer a range of crags and ridges suitable for climbers and abseilers. The Cobbler, or Ben Arthur, is a popular peak that provides a mix of rock climbing and scrambling, culminating in a rewarding summit. The stunning views of Loch Long and the surrounding area make it a memorable climbing destination.

5. Cairngorms National Park - Granite Playground:
The Cairngorms National Park features granite cliffs and boulders that attract climbers from around the world. The Shelter Stone Crag offers challenging routes, and the Northern Corries are known for their winter climbing opportunities. The park's varied landscapes provide a playground for climbers of all skill levels.

6. Safety and Equipment:
Rock climbing and abseiling require proper equipment and safety measures. It's essential to have the right gear, including harnesses, helmets, ropes, and appropriate footwear. Beginners should

consider hiring experienced guides or joining climbing courses to learn the necessary skills and techniques for a safe and enjoyable experience.

Scotland's diverse and awe-inspiring landscapes provide an ideal setting for rock climbing and abseiling adventures. Whether you're scaling majestic mountains, tackling challenging ridges, or exploring sea stacks along the rugged coastline, Scotland's varied terrain offers something for every climbing enthusiast. With proper preparation, respect for the environment, and a spirit of adventure, you'll be rewarded with unforgettable memories and a deep appreciation for Scotland's natural wonders.

7.7 Ski Resorts in the Scottish Highlands

The Scottish Highlands offer a winter playground like no other, with stunning landscapes, pristine snow-covered peaks, and a range of ski resorts that cater to snow enthusiasts of all levels. From beginners to seasoned skiers and snowboarders, the Scottish Highlands provide a unique opportunity to experience winter sports against a backdrop of rugged beauty. With a mix of challenging slopes, cozy lodges, and breathtaking views, the ski resorts in the Scottish Highlands promise an unforgettable winter getaway.

1. Glencoe Mountain Resort:
Nestled in the iconic Glencoe Valley, this resort is known for its dramatic scenery and diverse terrain. Offering a variety of slopes, including wide-open runs and challenging black diamond trails, Glencoe Mountain Resort caters to skiers and snowboarders of different skill levels. The resort's off-piste opportunities and stunning vistas make it a favorite among winter sports enthusiasts.

2. Nevis Range Mountain Resort:
Located on the slopes of Aonach Mor near Ben Nevis, Nevis Range offers a wide range of skiing and snowboarding experiences. The Back Corries are known for their challenging terrain, while the Aonach Mor Gondola provides access to gentler slopes suitable for beginners and families. The resort's unique tree line and breathtaking views of the Great Glen make it an unforgettable destination.

3. CairnGorm Mountain:
CairnGorm Mountain is one of Scotland's most popular ski resorts, offering a mix of slopes for all abilities. The funicular railway takes visitors to the Ptarmigan Top Station, providing access to various runs and panoramic views. The resort's terrain

parks and extensive beginner areas make it a great choice for families and beginners.

4. Glenshee Ski Centre:
Known as the "Glen of the Fairies," Glenshee Ski Centre is the largest ski resort in Scotland, boasting a staggering 22 lifts and 36 runs across three valleys. With terrain suitable for all levels, from gentle beginner slopes to challenging black runs, Glenshee offers a diverse skiing and snowboarding experience. The resort's expansive space and wide variety of slopes make it a great destination for groups of varying abilities.

5. Lecht 2090:
Lecht 2090 is a family-friendly ski resort that focuses on providing a welcoming environment for beginners and families. The resort features gentle slopes, a snow park for children, and ski schools for those new to winter sports. Its emphasis on learning and family fun makes Lecht 2090 an ideal destination for those looking to introduce their loved ones to skiing and snowboarding.

6. Après-Ski and Accommodation:
After a day on the slopes, the Scottish Highlands offer cozy lodges, charming cottages, and comfortable hotels where you can unwind. Many

resorts have on-site cafes, restaurants, and bars for après-ski relaxation. You can also explore nearby villages and towns to experience traditional Scottish hospitality and cuisine.

The ski resorts in the Scottish Highlands provide an incredible winter experience for skiers and snowboarders of all levels. From the breathtaking landscapes and challenging runs to the cozy accommodations and warm après-ski atmosphere, the Scottish Highlands offer a winter wonderland that's waiting to be explored. Whether you're seeking thrills on the slopes or a peaceful mountain retreat, the ski resorts in the Scottish Highlands offer a truly unforgettable winter getaway.

CHAPTER 8. Family-Friendly Accommodations

8.1 Family-Friendly Hotels and Resorts

Scotland is a destination that welcomes families with open arms, offering a wide range of family-friendly hotels and resorts that cater to the needs and preferences of travelers of all ages. From charming countryside retreats to coastal escapes and city adventures, Scotland's family-friendly accommodations provide comfort, convenience, and a plethora of activities to create lasting memories for your loved ones.

1. Cameron House Resort, Loch Lomond:
Nestled on the shores of Loch Lomond, Cameron House Resort offers a luxurious family escape with a variety of accommodations, including spacious lodges and family suites. Children can enjoy outdoor activities, including bike rides, Segway tours, and water sports on the loch, while parents indulge in spa treatments or rounds of golf.

2. Crieff Hydro, Perthshire:
Known as a family-focused resort, Crieff Hydro in Perthshire offers an array of activities for all ages. With an indoor pool, soft play area, and outdoor adventure zone, children will be entertained

throughout their stay. The resort's family rooms and self-catering lodges provide comfortable accommodations for families of all sizes.

3. Macdonald Aviemore Resort, Cairngorms:
Located in the heart of the Cairngorms National Park, this resort is a haven for outdoor enthusiasts. Families can explore the stunning surroundings, take part in activities like skiing, snowboarding, and hiking, and then retreat to spacious family-friendly lodges or suites. The resort's swimming pool, cinema, and play areas ensure entertainment for everyone.

4. Gleneagles, Perthshire:
Gleneagles is a luxury resort that caters to families seeking elegance and adventure. With supervised kids' clubs, family-friendly dining options, and activities such as horseback riding and falconry, Gleneagles offers a memorable escape. The resort's estate rooms and suites provide a comfortable base for your family retreat.

5. Marine Hotel, North Berwick:
For families looking to explore Scotland's stunning coastline, Marine Hotel in North Berwick offers a beachside escape. Family rooms with sea views, a

kids' club, and nearby attractions like the Scottish Seabird Centre make it an ideal choice for families seeking a coastal adventure.

6. City Breaks: Apex Grassmarket, Edinburgh:

If you're planning a city break in Edinburgh, the Apex Grassmarket Hotel is a family-friendly choice. Its central location allows for easy access to the city's attractions, while family rooms and suites provide ample space for everyone. Explore Edinburgh Castle, the Royal Mile, and other family-friendly sites within walking distance.

7. Family-Friendly Amenities:

Family-friendly hotels and resorts in Scotland go the extra mile to ensure that both parents and children have a comfortable and enjoyable stay. Look for accommodations that offer amenities such as children's menus, play areas, babysitting services, and family-sized rooms or suites.

Scotland's family-friendly hotels and resorts provide a haven for families looking to create unforgettable memories together. From outdoor adventures in the Highlands to coastal explorations and city escapades, these accommodations cater to travelers of all ages. With comfortable accommodations, a range of activities, and amenities designed to make your family feel at home, Scotland offers a wealth of options for a perfect family getaway.

8.2 Self-Catering Cottages and Apartments

When it comes to experiencing the beauty and charm of Scotland, self-catering cottages and apartments offer a unique and flexible way to immerse yourself in the local culture and landscapes. From charming cottages nestled in the countryside to modern apartments in vibrant cities, self-catering accommodations provide travelers with the freedom to explore at their own pace while enjoying the comfort of a home away from home.

1. Rural Retreats:
Escape the hustle and bustle of city life by staying in a self-catering cottage in the Scottish countryside. These quaint cottages often feature traditional architecture and are surrounded by picturesque landscapes. Whether it's a cottage by a tranquil loch, nestled in the rolling hills, or near a quaint village, you'll have the opportunity to disconnect and enjoy a peaceful retreat.

2. Coastal Getaways:

Scotland's stunning coastline offers a variety of self-catering options, from charming seaside cottages to modern apartments with ocean views. Imagine waking up to the sound of waves crashing and exploring rugged cliffs or sandy beaches just steps away from your accommodation.

3. City Apartments:

For those seeking the vibrancy of Scotland's cities, self-catering apartments provide a convenient base for urban explorations. Whether it's the historic charm of Edinburgh, the cultural hub of Glasgow, or the maritime allure of Aberdeen, you can find apartments in the heart of the action.

4. Flexibility and Freedom:

One of the main advantages of self-catering accommodations is the flexibility they offer. With a fully equipped kitchen, you can choose to prepare your own meals using local produce, giving you a taste of Scotland's culinary delights. This flexibility is particularly beneficial for families, groups, or those with dietary restrictions.

5. Local Experiences:

Staying in a self-catering cottage or apartment allows you to connect with the local community on a deeper level. Visit nearby markets, chat with neighbors, and experience daily life in Scotland firsthand. This immersive experience provides insight into the culture, traditions, and way of life that make Scotland unique.

6. Tips for Booking:
When booking self-catering accommodations in Scotland, consider the following:

  - Location: Decide whether you want a rural, coastal, or city setting based on your preferences and travel itinerary.

  - Size: Choose a cottage or apartment that suits the size of your group, whether you're traveling as a couple, a family, or a larger group.

  - Amenities: Check the amenities provided, such as Wi-Fi, parking, laundry facilities, and any extras like fireplaces or outdoor spaces.

  - Availability: Self-catering accommodations can be in high demand, especially during peak seasons. Book well in advance to secure your preferred dates and location.

Self-catering cottages and apartments in Scotland offer a personalized and immersive way to experience the country's diverse landscapes and culture. Whether you're seeking a tranquil rural retreat, a coastal haven, or an urban adventure, these accommodations provide a comfortable and flexible home base for your Scottish journey. Embrace the freedom to explore, connect with the local community, and create cherished memories in a home away from home.

8.3 Glamping and Camping Sites

Title: Glamping and Camping Adventures in Scotland: Embrace Nature in Comfort

Introduction:
Scotland's breathtaking landscapes, from rolling hills to rugged coastlines, provide the perfect backdrop for outdoor enthusiasts seeking a unique camping experience. Glamping and camping sites offer a way to immerse yourself in nature while enjoying the comforts of modern amenities. Whether you're looking to disconnect in a remote wilderness or explore the charm of Scotland's lochs and forests, glamping and camping sites in Scotland promise unforgettable adventures.

1. Glamping: Where Comfort Meets Nature:
Glamping, a fusion of "glamorous" and "camping," offers a luxurious twist to traditional camping.

Accommodations range from yurts and safari tents to eco pods and treehouses. Glamping sites in Scotland provide cozy beds, heating, and sometimes en-suite bathrooms, ensuring a comfortable stay while surrounded by nature.

2. Camping: Traditional Adventure:
For those seeking a more traditional camping experience, Scotland offers a wide variety of camping sites. From designated campsites with facilities to wild camping in remote areas, camping enthusiasts can pitch their tents amidst stunning landscapes.

3. Loch Lomond and Trossachs National Park:
The picturesque Loch Lomond and Trossachs National Park is a popular destination for glamping and camping. With a mix of lochside campsites, remote glamping sites, and charming cabins, visitors can enjoy activities such as kayaking, hiking, and wildlife watching while experiencing the beauty of the Scottish wilderness.

4. Cairngorms National Park:
The Cairngorms National Park offers a range of glamping options, including wooden pods, shepherd's huts, and tipis. Set against the backdrop of the Cairngorms Mountains, visitors can explore

the park's trails, spot wildlife, and indulge in stargazing in some of the darkest skies in Europe.

5. Isle of Skye:
The rugged landscapes of the Isle of Skye provide a unique setting for glamping and camping. With cozy pods and lodges available, visitors can explore the island's dramatic coastline, waterfalls, and iconic landmarks like the Old Man of Storr.

6. Tips for a Memorable Experience:
When considering glamping and camping in Scotland, keep the following in mind:

- Season: Check the best time to visit, as Scotland's weather can be unpredictable. Summer offers longer daylight hours and milder temperatures.

- Booking: Glamping sites often require advance booking due to their popularity. Reserve your accommodation well in advance, especially during peak seasons.

- Equipment: Depending on the type of glamping or camping you choose, you may need to bring camping gear. Check with the site for provided amenities.

- Regulations: Be aware of camping regulations, especially if you plan to wild camp. Follow the "Leave No Trace" principles to minimize your impact on the environment.

Glamping and camping sites in Scotland offer a chance to connect with nature in a comfortable and immersive way. Whether you're drawn to the luxury of glamping accommodations or the simplicity of traditional camping, Scotland's diverse landscapes provide endless opportunities for adventure and relaxation. From the tranquility of lochs to the majesty of mountains, glamping and camping in Scotland promise unforgettable experiences and a deep connection to the natural world.

8.4 Farm Stays and Rural Retreats

Farm stays and rural retreats have gained immense popularity in recent years as travelers seek unique and authentic experiences away from the hustle and bustle of urban life. Scotland, with its breathtaking landscapes, rich history, and warm hospitality, offers a perfect setting for those looking to escape to the countryside. In this training guide, we'll delve extensively into the world of farm stays and rural retreats in Scotland, highlighting their benefits, features, and how to make the most of these experiences.

Benefits of Farm Stays and Rural Retreats in Scotland:

1. Connection with Nature: Farm stays and rural retreats provide an opportunity to immerse oneself in the natural beauty of Scotland's countryside. From rolling hills to serene lochs, these locations offer stunning vistas that can be truly rejuvenating.

2. Authentic Experience: Staying on a farm or in a rural setting allows visitors to experience the authentic way of life in Scotland. Engaging in daily farm activities, interacting with locals, and participating in traditional rituals offer insights into the country's culture.

3. Tranquility and Relaxation: The serene environment of the countryside offers a peaceful retreat away from the noise and stress of urban living. The tranquility allows for relaxation and introspection.

4. Outdoor Activities: Farm stays often provide access to various outdoor activities such as hiking, fishing, and horseback riding. This is a great way to explore the natural beauty of Scotland firsthand.

5. Farm-to-Table Experience: Many farm stays offer farm-fresh meals, providing visitors with an authentic farm-to-table culinary experience. This allows for a taste of local produce and traditional dishes.

Features of Farm Stays and Rural Retreats:
1. Accommodation Variety: Accommodations range from cozy cottages and converted barns to luxurious farmhouses. This variety caters to different preferences and budgets.

2. Hands-On Activities: Visitors can partake in activities like milking cows, collecting eggs, and helping with seasonal farming tasks. These interactions foster a sense of involvement and learning.

3. Local Workshops: Some farm stays offer workshops on traditional crafts, cooking, and local traditions, allowing visitors to engage with Scottish culture on a deeper level.

4. Petting Farms: Many places have petting farms where guests can interact with friendly animals, making it an ideal family-friendly experience.

5. Scenic Trails: Rural retreats often have walking trails that lead to stunning viewpoints, historical sites, and charming villages, enabling guests to explore the surroundings.

Making the Most of Your Experience:
1. Research: Before booking, research different farm stays and rural retreats to find the one that aligns with your preferences and interests.

2. Pack Accordingly: As rural locations might have varying weather conditions, pack appropriately for outdoor activities and changing temperatures.

3. Engage with Locals: Take the opportunity to chat with the farm owners and locals. They can provide insights into the region's history, culture, and hidden gems.

4. Disconnect: Embrace the chance to disconnect from technology and fully immerse yourself in the natural surroundings.

5. Respect Nature: Remember that you are a guest in a natural environment. Respect the flora, fauna, and local wildlife during your stay.

Exploring farm stays and rural retreats in Scotland offers a unique and enriching experience that combines the tranquility of the countryside with authentic cultural immersion. From connecting with nature to participating in farm activities, these retreats provide a memorable way to experience the heart and soul of Scotland. By understanding their benefits, features, and how to make the most of your stay, you can embark on a journey that is not only enjoyable but also deeply meaningful.

8.5 Hotels with Kids' Clubs and Playgrounds

Traveling with children can be a rewarding experience, but it often requires careful planning to ensure that everyone has a memorable and enjoyable time. Scotland, with its stunning landscapes and rich cultural heritage, offers an array of family-friendly accommodations that cater to the needs of both parents and children. In this comprehensive travel guide, we'll explore the world of hotels with kids' clubs and playgrounds in Scotland, highlighting their advantages, features, and tips for making the most of your family vacation.

Advantages of Hotels with Kids' Clubs and Playgrounds:

Engaging Activities: Kids' clubs offer a range of supervised activities that keep children entertained and engaged, giving parents some well-deserved relaxation time.

Social Interaction: Children have the chance to interact with peers, make new friends, and develop social skills in a safe and controlled environment.

Parental Relaxation: Parents can unwind and enjoy some quality time together while their children are occupied with age-appropriate activities.

Educational Opportunities: Many kids' clubs incorporate educational elements into their programs, allowing children to learn while having fun.

Convenience: Hotels with kids' clubs and playgrounds provide a convenient option for families, as parents can easily keep an eye on their children while still enjoying the hotel's amenities.

Features of Hotels with Kids' Clubs and Playgrounds:

Diverse Accommodations: From luxurious resorts to charming countryside inns, Scotland offers a range of family-friendly accommodations with kids' clubs and playgrounds.

Age-Appropriate Activities: Kids' clubs often tailor their activities to different age groups, ensuring that children are engaged and entertained based on their developmental stage.

Outdoor Playgrounds: Many hotels feature outdoor playgrounds equipped with swings, slides, climbing structures, and even nature trails, providing children with a safe space to explore and play.

Indoor Play Areas: In case of inclement weather, indoor play areas within the hotel premises offer a haven for children to enjoy games, crafts, and other indoor activities.

Themed Programs: Some hotels design themed kids' club programs that revolve around local culture, wildlife, or history, making the learning experience exciting for children.

Tips for Maximizing Your Family Vacation:

Research: Look for hotels that offer well-reviewed kids' clubs and playgrounds that match your family's preferences and needs.

Pack Accordingly: Pack essentials for both indoor and outdoor activities, including appropriate clothing and shoes for various weather conditions.

Schedule Rest Time: While engaging in activities is important, make sure to schedule downtime for your children to rest and recharge.

Participate Together: Some hotels offer family-oriented activities where parents can join in the fun alongside their children, creating lasting memories.

Explore Nearby Attractions: Take advantage of the hotel's location by exploring nearby family-friendly attractions, ensuring a well-rounded vacation experience.

Choosing a hotel with a kids' club and playground in Scotland can greatly enhance your family vacation by providing a balance of relaxation, entertainment, and educational experiences. With diverse accommodations and a variety of features, these family-friendly hotels offer a convenient and enjoyable way to explore Scotland's natural beauty and cultural heritage while ensuring that both parents and children have a memorable getaway.

8.6 Pet-Friendly Accommodations

Scotland, with its stunning landscapes, historic sites, and vibrant culture, is an ideal destination for travelers looking to explore its beauty with their furry companions. Finding pet-friendly accommodations can be a crucial aspect of planning your trip. This guide aims to provide you with an extensive list of pet-friendly options, ranging from charming cottages to luxurious hotels, ensuring that both you and your four-legged friend have an unforgettable experience.

1. Charming Cottages:

For a cozy and homey experience, consider staying in a charming cottage. Many cottages throughout Scotland welcome pets, allowing them to explore the surrounding countryside with you. Places like the Scottish Highlands offer a plethora of cottages that provide comfort and a warm atmosphere, giving you and your pet a serene retreat.

2. Seaside Retreats:

Scotland's breathtaking coastline offers numerous pet-friendly accommodations where you and your furry friend can enjoy walks along the beach and stunning ocean views. From quaint fishing villages to lively coastal towns, you'll find a range of options that cater to pet owners.

3. Countryside Retreats:

Escape the hustle and bustle of city life by opting for a countryside retreat. Scotland's rural areas boast a variety of pet-friendly lodges and guesthouses, providing a peaceful environment for you and your pet to relax and unwind.

4. Pet-Friendly Hotels:

Several hotels in Scotland are dedicated to ensuring that your pet has a comfortable stay. These establishments often provide amenities like pet beds, food bowls, and even special treats for your furry companion. Many hotels are conveniently located near parks or nature reserves, making it easy to take your pet for a leisurely stroll.

5. Glamping with Pets:

Experience the beauty of the Scottish outdoors while enjoying the comforts of glamping. Many glamping sites allow pets and offer unique accommodations such as luxury tents, yurts, and cabins. This option provides a blend of nature and luxury that you and your pet can both enjoy.

6. Practical Considerations:

When booking pet-friendly accommodations, it's essential to consider the specific needs of your pet. Check if the establishment has any restrictions on the size or breed of pets, as well as any additional fees. Additionally, inquire about nearby pet-friendly attractions, such as parks, trails, and cafes, to ensure a well-rounded experience for both you and your furry friend.

7. Etiquette and Responsibility:

While staying at pet-friendly accommodations, it's crucial to be a responsible pet owner. Always clean up after your pet, keep them on a leash where required, and be mindful of other guests. By being considerate, you contribute to a positive experience for everyone.

8. Booking Tips:

Plan Ahead: As pet-friendly accommodations can be in high demand, especially during peak seasons, make your reservations well in advance to secure your preferred lodging.

Read Reviews: Before booking, read reviews from other pet owners who have stayed at the accommodation. Their insights can provide valuable information about the suitability of the place for your pet.

Scotland offers a wide range of pet-friendly accommodations, ensuring that you and your beloved pet can enjoy the beauty and charm of this remarkable country together.

CHAPTER 9. Romantic and Cozy Lodgings for Couples

9.1 Boutique Hotels with Romantic Ambiance

Scotland's breathtaking landscapes and rich history set the stage for an unforgettable romantic getaway. If you're seeking an intimate escape with your loved one, look no further than the country's collection of boutique hotels that offer an ambiance of romance like no other. From charming countryside retreats to elegant city sanctuaries, these boutique hotels in Scotland are designed to create lasting memories for couples seeking to rekindle their love or celebrate special occasions.

1. The Witchery by the Castle - Edinburgh: Nestled in the heart of Edinburgh's historic Old Town, The Witchery by the Castle is a decadent and luxurious boutique hotel that exudes an air of mystique and romance. Indulge in opulent suites adorned with antique furniture, tapestries, and lavish fabrics. The hotel's acclaimed restaurant serves sumptuous Scottish cuisine in a candlelit setting, making it an ideal spot for a romantic dinner.

2. Knockinaam Lodge - Dumfries and Galloway:

Tucked away on the rugged coastline of Dumfries and Galloway, Knockinaam Lodge offers seclusion and intimacy like no other. With only ten individually designed rooms, this charming country house hotel provides an idyllic backdrop for couples. Take romantic strolls along the private beach, enjoy candlelit dinners, and unwind in rooms with stunning sea views.

3. Cromlix - Perthshire:

Owned by tennis legend Andy Murray, Cromlix is a five-star Victorian mansion turned boutique hotel. Set amidst lush gardens and woodlands in Perthshire, this elegant retreat offers an intimate escape. From its luxurious suites to the Chez Roux restaurant by renowned chef Albert Roux, every detail is meticulously crafted for a romantic experience.

4. Inverlochy Castle Hotel - Fort William:

Situated amidst the dramatic landscapes of the Scottish Highlands, Inverlochy Castle Hotel offers a fairytale-like ambiance for couples seeking a romantic escape. This 19th-century castle-turned-hotel boasts regal suites, fine dining at the Albert and Michel Roux Jr. restaurant, and opportunities for outdoor adventures in the surrounding wilderness.

5. Fonab Castle Hotel & Spa - Pitlochry:
Overlooking the serene Loch Faskally, Fonab Castle Hotel & Spa is a luxurious haven for couples seeking both relaxation and adventure. With its contemporary design juxtaposed against the castle's historic façade, this boutique hotel offers lavish suites, a spa with couples' treatments, and opportunities for watersports on the loch.

Scotland's boutique hotels with romantic ambiance provide the perfect backdrop for couples to celebrate love and create cherished memories. Whether you're exploring the charming streets of Edinburgh, wandering along rugged coastlines, or immersing yourselves in the Highlands' beauty, these enchanting hotels promise an unforgettable romantic experience. From luxurious furnishings to intimate dining experiences, each boutique hotel mentioned here is a testament to Scotland's ability to ignite and rekindle the flames of romance.

9.2 Luxury Resorts and Spas

Scotland, known for its rich history, stunning landscapes, and warm hospitality, is also home to a collection of world-class luxury resorts and spas that redefine indulgence. If you're seeking a getaway that blends opulence with tranquility, these luxurious destinations promise an unforgettable experience. From the serene shores of lochs to the majestic Highlands, these luxury resorts and spas in Scotland offer an unparalleled escape for those seeking relaxation, rejuvenation, and refined comfort.

1. Gleneagles - Perthshire:

Nestled in the heart of Perthshire's rolling hills, Gleneagles is an iconic luxury resort that offers a blend of classic elegance and modern amenities. With its five-star accommodations, three championship golf courses, and an award-winning spa, Gleneagles caters to both relaxation and recreation. The spa features an array of treatments inspired by the surrounding nature, providing a holistic wellness experience.

2. Cameron House - Loch Lomond:

Set on the shores of Loch Lomond, Cameron House is a picturesque luxury resort that showcases the beauty of the Scottish Highlands. This retreat boasts elegant rooms, gourmet dining options, and a spa that overlooks the serene loch. Guests can indulge in treatments using organic ingredients and enjoy the rooftop infinity pool with breathtaking views.

3. The Machrie Hotel & Golf Links - Isle of Islay:

For those seeking luxury in a remote and pristine setting, The Machrie Hotel & Golf Links on the Isle of Islay is a perfect choice. This modern resort offers luxurious accommodations, a championship golf course, and a spa that focuses on holistic wellness. The tranquil surroundings and coastal vistas create an atmosphere of pure relaxation.

4. Fonab Castle Hotel & Spa - Pitlochry:

Perched on the banks of Loch Faskally, Fonab Castle Hotel & Spa is a masterpiece of contemporary luxury within a historic castle setting. The resort boasts luxurious rooms, a spa with rejuvenating treatments, and a fine-dining restaurant. Guests can unwind while enjoying the breathtaking views of the loch and surrounding landscapes.

5. The Balmoral - Edinburgh:

Located in the heart of Edinburgh, The Balmoral is a landmark luxury hotel that offers an urban retreat like no other. With its elegant rooms, Michelin-starred dining, and a spa that draws inspiration from Scotland's landscapes, this hotel seamlessly blends city sophistication with relaxation.

6. Achnagairn Castle - Inverness:
Achnagairn Castle presents a unique blend of historic charm and modern luxury. This exclusive-use castle boasts opulent suites, lavish interiors, and an in-house spa. The castle's grounds provide a serene backdrop for relaxation, and its proximity to Inverness offers opportunities for exploration.

Scotland's luxury resorts and spas redefine the concept of indulgence, offering a blend of opulence, natural beauty, and holistic wellness. Whether you're seeking a serene escape by the lochs, an adventure in the Highlands, or an urban retreat in Edinburgh, these destinations promise a lavish experience that lingers in memory. From championship golf courses to serene spas, each luxury resort mentioned here is a testament to Scotland's ability to create a haven of luxury amid its breathtaking landscapes.

9.3 Secluded Cottages and Cabins

Escape the hustle and bustle of everyday life and immerse yourself in the tranquil beauty of

Scotland's secluded cottages and cabins. Tucked away amidst rugged landscapes, these hidden gems offer a unique opportunity to disconnect, rejuvenate, and reconnect with nature. Whether you're seeking a romantic retreat or a peaceful solo getaway, these secluded accommodations promise an intimate experience surrounded by Scotland's breathtaking scenery.

1. The Old Mill Cottage - Isle of Skye:
Nestled on the enchanting Isle of Skye, The Old Mill Cottage is a charming stone cottage that offers seclusion and serenity. With its rustic interiors and stunning views of rolling hills, this cottage is perfect for couples looking to escape into nature. Explore nearby hiking trails, enjoy quiet evenings by the fireplace, and revel in the island's mystical beauty.

2. Eagle Brae - Highlands:
Immerse yourself in the untamed wilderness of the Scottish Highlands at Eagle Brae. This collection of handcrafted log cabins seamlessly blends luxury with nature. Each cabin is unique, featuring traditional craftsmanship, modern amenities, and panoramic views. Set amidst the Glen Affric Nature Reserve, Eagle Brae offers a chance to encounter wildlife, hike through ancient forests, and stargaze under clear Highland skies.

3. The Tree Howf - Perthshire:

Experience the magic of a treetop retreat at The Tree Howf in Perthshire. This innovative cabin, perched among the branches, offers unparalleled seclusion and an immersive nature experience. With a wood-fired hot tub and stunning views, it's an ideal spot for a romantic escape. Disconnect from the world and reconnect with your surroundings in this hidden haven.

4. Ardanaiseig Boat Shed - Argyll and Bute:

Situated on the shores of Loch Awe, the Ardanaiseig Boat Shed is a charming and remote cottage that combines waterfront living with privacy. Accessible only by boat, this rustic hideaway offers an escape from the ordinary. Enjoy fishing, boating, and the simple pleasures of lakeside living, all while surrounded by the tranquility of the loch and forest.

5. The Sheiling - Cairngorms National Park:

For those seeking a mountain retreat, The Sheiling in Cairngorms National Park is a cozy cabin that offers panoramic views of the surrounding peaks. This eco-friendly cabin provides an intimate space to unwind, hike through the Cairngorms, and witness the beauty of changing landscapes in every season.

6. Lazy Duck - Nethy Bridge:
Set in a forested area near Nethy Bridge, the Lazy
Duck offers a range of secluded accommodations,
from wooden cabins to a converted mill house.
Embrace the simple life with wood-fired saunas,
outdoor showers, and the soothing sounds of the
nearby river. This tranquil retreat encourages you
to disconnect and immerse yourself in nature.

Scotland's secluded cottages and cabins provide the
perfect escape for those seeking solitude and a deep
connection with nature. From island getaways to
mountain retreats, these hidden accommodations
offer an opportunity to step away from the demands
of modern life and embrace the tranquility and
beauty of Scotland's landscapes. Whether it's the
rugged coastline, mist-covered hills, or pristine
forests, each location mentioned here promises an
unforgettable and secluded experience.

9.4 Castle Stays and Historical Manors

Scotland's rich history and storied past come alive
through its magnificent castles and historical
manors, offering a unique opportunity for travelers
to step back in time while enjoying luxurious
accommodations. Whether perched on rugged
cliffs, nestled within lush landscapes, or gracing the

shores of serene lochs, these castle stays and historical manors invite guests to experience the grandeur of a bygone era while reveling in modern comfort.

1.Dalhousie Castle - Midlothian:

Dating back to the 13th century, Dalhousie Castle offers an enchanting experience just a stone's throw away from Edinburgh. Nestled amidst picturesque woodlands, this medieval fortress turned luxury hotel boasts luxurious rooms, a spa in the ancient vaults, and the captivating falconry experience that adds a touch of mystique to your stay.

2.Cameron House - Loch Lomond:

Situated on the banks of Loch Lomond, Cameron House seamlessly blends traditional Scottish elegance with modern luxury. The mansion offers sumptuous rooms, gourmet dining, and picturesque views. Explore the estate's grounds, enjoy water sports on the loch, and bask in the timeless beauty of the Scottish countryside.

3.Inveraray Castle - Argyll and Bute:

The ancestral home of the Duke of Argyll, Inveraray Castle is both a historic landmark and a charming bed and breakfast. Guests can stay in one of the castle's cozy rooms and enjoy guided tours of the castle during the day. The surrounding gardens and loch views add to the enchantment of this unique stay.

4.Ackergill Tower - Caithness:

Perched on the dramatic Caithness coastline, Ackergill Tower is a 15th-century castle that offers an intimate and luxurious escape. With opulent interiors, stunning sea views, and even a private beach, this castle provides a fairy-tale setting for weddings, romantic getaways, and special occasions.

5.Barony Castle - Scottish Borders:

Set in the tranquil Scottish Borders, Barony Castle is a historic manor house turned modern hotel that offers a mix of tradition and comfort. The castle's elegant rooms, spa facilities, and proximity to the rolling hills make it an ideal retreat for those seeking relaxation and exploration.

6. **Dornoch Castle Hotel - Dornoch:**
Located in the charming town of Dornoch, the Dornoch Castle Hotel immerses guests in Highland history. This 15th-century castle turned hotel offers cozy rooms, fine dining, and the chance to explore Dornoch's historic streets, renowned golf courses, and nearby beaches.

Castle stays and historical manors in Scotland offer a chance to immerse oneself in the country's rich heritage while indulging in luxurious accommodations and modern comforts. Whether you're gazing across serene lochs, exploring ancient halls, or simply enjoying the beauty of lush landscapes, each castle and manor mentioned here promises a timeless and unforgettable experience that transports you to a different era.

9.5 Romantic Bed and Breakfasts

Scotland's charming landscapes and warm hospitality create the perfect backdrop for a romantic escape. For couples seeking an intimate getaway, the country's collection of romantic bed and breakfasts offer a blend of coziness, personal touch, and picturesque surroundings. From quaint countryside retreats to coastal havens, these bed and breakfasts provide the ideal setting to kindle romance and create cherished memories.

1. Knoydart Hide - Knoydart:

Accessible only by boat or a hike, Knoydart Hide offers unparalleled seclusion for couples seeking privacy and tranquility. This intimate hideaway boasts luxurious accommodations, stunning loch views, and the chance to explore Knoydart's untouched wilderness together. Relax in a hot tub under starlit skies, and let the serenity of the surroundings deepen your connection.

2. Aberfeldy Weem Hotel - Perthshire:
Nestled in the heart of Perthshire, the Aberfeldy Weem Hotel exudes a sense of old-world charm and romance. With individually decorated rooms, a cozy bar, and a restaurant featuring locally sourced ingredients, this hotel offers an intimate atmosphere perfect for couples seeking relaxation and gourmet experiences.

3. Aikenshill House - Aberdeenshire:
Set amidst rolling hills and close to the North Sea, Aikenshill House is a luxurious bed and breakfast that offers a serene escape. The elegant rooms, attentive hosts, and proximity to picturesque beaches make it an idyllic spot for a romantic retreat. Indulge in locally sourced breakfasts and leisurely walks along the coastline.

4. Achaban House - Isle of Mull:
Overlooking the Sound of Iona, Achaban House on the Isle of Mull radiates romance and tranquility. This Victorian villa offers charming rooms, a peaceful garden, and breathtaking sea views. Explore the island's rugged landscapes, visit

historic sites, and enjoy quiet evenings in this intimate haven.

5. The Bressay Lighthouse - Shetland Islands:

For a truly unique experience, The Bressay Lighthouse offers a romantic stay on the rugged Shetland Islands. The self-catering accommodations within the lighthouse tower provide unparalleled views of the surrounding seascape. Immerse yourselves in the island's natural beauty and embrace the isolation of this unforgettable getaway.

6. The Four Seasons - Stirling:

Situated near Stirling Castle, The Four Seasons is a boutique bed and breakfast that exudes warmth and elegance. The individually decorated rooms, attentive hosts, and proximity to historic landmarks create an enchanting ambiance for couples. Enjoy leisurely walks through Stirling's historic streets and cozy evenings in this charming retreat.

Scotland's romantic bed and breakfasts offer an intimate and personal touch that makes them ideal havens for couples in search of romantic getaways. Whether you're savoring breakfast in bed, exploring the rugged landscapes, or simply enjoying each other's company by the fireplace, each bed and breakfast mentioned here promises a unique and unforgettable experience that rekindles the flames of romance.

9.6 Unique and Quirky Accommodations

For travelers seeking an out-of-the-ordinary experience, Scotland offers a treasure trove of unique and quirky accommodations that promise to make your stay truly unforgettable. From sleeping in treehouses to spending the night in historic castles, these one-of-a-kind options allow you to immerse yourself in Scotland's rich history and breathtaking landscapes while indulging in a touch of whimsy and novelty.

1.The Glamping Village - Isle of Skye:
Experience the rugged beauty of the Isle of Skye from the comfort of a luxurious glamping pod. The Glamping Village offers a range of pods, each with its own theme and design. Whether you choose a pod with a hot tub or one inspired by traditional Scottish architecture, you'll wake up to stunning views and the serenity of nature.

2.The Witchery Suites - Edinburgh:
Located within Edinburgh's historic Old Town, The Witchery Suites offer opulent and theatrical

accommodations within a historic building. Each suite is uniquely designed with lavish decor, sumptuous fabrics, and an air of mystery. Immerse yourselves in the romantic ambiance of these suites while exploring the city's cobblestone streets.

3. The Jacobite Train - Highlands:
Step into the magical world of Harry Potter by staying aboard the Jacobite Train, famously known as the Hogwarts Express. This luxury train offers overnight accommodations with a vintage charm, sweeping views of the Highlands, and the nostalgia of a bygone era. Experience the enchantment of the Scottish landscape as you journey across iconic bridges and landscapes.

4.The Lost Pod - Cairngorms National Park:
For a truly off-the-grid experience, consider staying at The Lost Pod in Cairngorms National Park. This compact and eco-friendly pod offers panoramic views of the surrounding mountains. Disconnect from technology, immerse yourself in nature, and enjoy cozy nights under the starlit sky.

5.The Lodge on Loch Goil - Argyll:
Set against the backdrop of Loch Goil, The Lodge offers quirky accommodations within a luxurious and secluded setting. Choose from themed rooms

that range from "Alice in Wonderland" to "Out of Africa." Explore the enchanting gardens, take a boat trip on the loch, and let your imagination run wild in this whimsical retreat.

6.Converted Railway Carriages - Fife:
Relive the romance of train travel by staying in a converted railway carriage in Fife. These unique accommodations offer a blend of vintage charm and modern comfort. Wake up to stunning sea views and enjoy easy access to the coastal paths and beaches that characterize this charming region.

Scotland's unique and quirky accommodations invite you to embrace the extraordinary and create lasting memories. Whether you're sleeping in a treehouse, enjoying the luxury of a train carriage, or experiencing the magic of a themed suite, each option mentioned here promises an adventure that blends novelty, comfort, and Scotland's natural beauty.

CHAPTER 10. Safety and Travel Tips for Scotland

10.1 Health and Safety Guidelines

Certainly! When traveling to Scotland, it's important to be aware of the health and safety guidelines to ensure a safe and enjoyable trip. Scotland, like many other destinations, places a strong emphasis on the well-being of its residents and visitors. Here are some key health and safety guidelines to keep in mind:

1. COVID-19 Precautions: As of September 2021, COVID-19 guidelines are subject to change. It's crucial to stay updated on the latest travel advisories, entry requirements, and safety measures related to the pandemic. Check the official government websites or contact local authorities before your trip.

2. Emergency Services: Scotland has a reliable emergency service system. In case of any medical emergency, fire, or police assistance, dial 999 or 112. The operators will guide you through the necessary steps.

3. Healthcare Facilities: Scotland boasts a well-developed healthcare system. Visitors from the

European Economic Area (EEA) and Switzerland are usually entitled to free or reduced-cost emergency medical treatment, while others may need travel insurance to cover medical expenses. It's advisable to have comprehensive travel insurance that includes medical coverage.

4. Prescription Medications: If you're bringing prescription medications, make sure to carry them in their original packaging, accompanied by a copy of your prescription. Pharmacists are readily available to help with medication-related queries.

5. Outdoor Safety: Scotland's breathtaking landscapes are perfect for outdoor activities, but weather conditions can change rapidly. Always check weather forecasts before heading out and be prepared for rain or sudden drops in temperature. Wear appropriate clothing and footwear, and let someone know about your plans if you're heading into remote areas.

6. Traffic Rules: If you plan on driving in Scotland, remember that vehicles drive on the left side of the road. Seatbelts are mandatory for all passengers, and children must be in appropriate car seats. Follow speed limits and road signs diligently.

7. Food and Water Safety: Scotland's food hygiene standards are high. However, ensure that you consume food from reputable establishments. Tap water is safe to drink across the country.

8. Wildlife Awareness: Scotland is home to diverse wildlife, including deer, sheep, and various bird species. If you encounter wildlife, maintain a safe distance and avoid feeding them.

9. Coastal Safety: If you're planning activities along the coastline, be aware of tide times and potential risks associated with tides and currents. Familiarize yourself with local safety guidelines for water-related activities.

10. Cultural Sensitivity: While not directly related to health and safety, it's important to respect local customs and traditions. This includes being mindful of appropriate attire when visiting religious sites and demonstrating respect for local communities.

Remember that guidelines and regulations can evolve, so it's essential to stay updated with the latest information before and during your trip. Scotland's natural beauty and warm hospitality await you – just be sure to prioritize your health and safety every step of the way.

10.2 Emergency Contacts and Services

Sure, I'd be happy to provide you with information on emergency contacts and services in Scotland for your travel guide:

Emergency Services:
1. Police: In case of non-emergency situations or general assistance, you can contact the Police Service of Scotland at 101. For emergencies, dial 999.

2. Fire and Rescue: If you need help with a fire-related emergency, contact the Scottish Fire and Rescue Service at 999.

3. Ambulance: For medical emergencies, dial 999 to request an ambulance. The Scottish Ambulance Service will respond promptly to provide medical assistance.

Healthcare:
1. NHS (National Health Service): Scotland has a publicly funded healthcare system. In non-emergency medical situations, you can visit a local NHS clinic or hospital. In case of emergency, you can access medical care through Accident & Emergency (A&E) departments in hospitals.

Emergency Contacts:
1. Emergency Services: As mentioned above, for police, fire, and ambulance services, call 999 in case of an emergency.

2. Non-Emergency Police: If you require non-emergency police assistance or want to report a crime, call 101.

3. NHS 24: For medical advice when your situation is not life-threatening but you need guidance, you can call NHS 24 at 111. They provide healthcare advice 24/7.

Embassies and Consulates:
If you're a foreign traveler, it's also a good idea to have the contact information of your country's embassy or consulate in Scotland. They can provide assistance in case of lost passports, legal issues, or emergencies.

Mountain and Water Safety:
If you plan to engage in outdoor activities like hiking or water sports, remember that Scotland's landscape can be challenging. Always check weather forecasts, inform someone about your plans, and adhere to safety guidelines. In

mountainous areas, the Mountain Rescue service (dial 999) can assist if you encounter difficulties.

Travel Insurance:
Before your trip, consider purchasing travel insurance that covers medical emergencies, trip cancellations, and other unforeseen events. This can provide you with financial protection and peace of mind during your travels.

Remember, these services are there to ensure your safety during your trip to Scotland. It's wise to familiarize yourself with these contacts and services before you travel, so you're well-prepared in case of any unexpected situations.

10.3 Currency and Money Matters

Currency:
The official currency of Scotland is the British Pound Sterling (£), often simply referred to as the pound. The currency is denoted by the symbol "£" and is further divided into 100 smaller units called pence (singular: penny). You'll find both banknotes and coins in circulation.

Banknotes:
One unique aspect of Scottish currency is the issuance of its own banknotes by three Scottish

banks: the Bank of Scotland, the Royal Bank of Scotland (RBS), and Clydesdale Bank. These banknotes have distinctive designs and are widely accepted across Scotland. However, they might not be as readily accepted in other parts of the United Kingdom. English banknotes are also accepted in Scotland.

Coins:

Coins in Scotland are similar to those in the rest of the UK. They come in denominations of 1p, 2p, 5p, 10p, 20p, 50p, £1, and £2. Pound coins and smaller denominations are often used for day-to-day transactions, while larger notes are more commonly used for larger purchases.

ATMs and Banking:

ATMs (cash machines) are widely available in cities, towns, and tourist areas throughout Scotland. Major credit and debit cards are widely accepted for payment in restaurants, shops, and hotels. However, it's a good idea to carry some cash for smaller establishments or places that might not accept cards.

Currency Exchange:

If you're carrying foreign currency, you can exchange it for British Pounds at banks, currency exchange bureaus, or even some larger hotels. Keep in mind that exchange rates can vary, and some places might charge a commission for currency exchange. It's a good idea to compare rates before making a transaction.

Tipping:
Tipping is customary in Scotland. In restaurants, it's common to leave a tip of around 10-15% of the bill if a service charge hasn't already been added. In pubs and cafes, rounding up the bill is appreciated. Tipping for good service is also customary for services like taxis, hotel staff, and tour guides.

Credit and Debit Cards:
Major credit and debit cards such as Visa, MasterCard, and American Express are widely accepted. However, some smaller establishments might only accept cash. Make sure to inform your bank of your travel plans to avoid any issues with using your cards abroad.

Travel Insurance:
Before traveling to Scotland, consider purchasing travel insurance that covers medical expenses, trip cancellations, and any unexpected incidents. This will provide you with financial protection and peace of mind during your trip.

Currency and Money Safety:
To ensure the safety of your money, consider using a money belt or a secure wallet. It's also a good practice to keep a photocopy or digital scan of important documents like your passport and credit cards in case they're lost or stolen.

By understanding the local currency, payment options, and cultural practices related to money matters, you'll be well-prepared to navigate Scotland's financial landscape.

CHAPTER 11. Packing List and Essential Items

11.1 Clothing and Weather-Appropriate Gear

Scotland's breathtaking landscapes, rich history, and vibrant cities make it a top destination for travelers. However, its notoriously unpredictable weather can catch visitors off guard. To fully enjoy your Scottish adventure, it's crucial to pack the right clothing and gear for all types of weather. From the misty Highlands to the bustling streets of Edinburgh, here's a comprehensive guide to dressing appropriately for Scotland's ever-changing weather.

1. Layers are Key:
Scotland's weather can transition rapidly from sunshine to rain, wind, and even snow, all in the same day. Packing a variety of clothing layers allows you to adapt to these changes seamlessly. Start with a moisture-wicking base layer to keep you dry, add an insulating layer for warmth, and top it off with a waterproof and windproof outer layer to stay protected from the elements.

2. Waterproof Outerwear:

A reliable waterproof jacket is arguably the most important item in your Scotland travel wardrobe. Look for a jacket with taped seams and a hood to ensure complete protection from rain. Breathability is also essential to prevent sweating, so choose a jacket with good ventilation options.

3. Sturdy Footwear:
Comfortable, waterproof, and sturdy footwear is a must. Whether you're exploring the rugged trails of the Highlands or strolling through cobblestone streets, a pair of waterproof hiking boots or all-weather sneakers will keep your feet dry and supported.

4. Warm Accessories:
Don't forget accessories like hats, gloves, and scarves, especially if you're visiting during the colder months. These items not only provide warmth but also protect against wind chill. Opt for materials like wool or fleece for maximum insulation.

5. Convertible Clothing:
Packing convertible clothing items, such as pants that can be converted into shorts or shirts with roll-up sleeves, can be incredibly practical. They

allow you to adapt to sudden changes in temperature throughout the day.

6. Umbrella or Poncho:
While a good waterproof jacket is essential, having a compact travel umbrella or a poncho can provide extra coverage during heavy rain. This can be particularly useful when exploring cities or attending outdoor events.

7. Quick-Drying Fabrics:
Choose clothing made from quick-drying fabrics, such as nylon or polyester, which are perfect for layering and can handle sudden rain showers without leaving you uncomfortable for the rest of the day.

8. Weather-Resistant Accessories:
Protect your electronics, cameras, and other valuable items with weather-resistant bags or cases. Scotland's weather can be unpredictable, and having the right gear will ensure your belongings stay safe and functional.

9. Check Local Forecasts:
Before heading out for the day's activities, check the local weather forecast. This will help you plan your outfit and gear accordingly. Remember that

weather conditions can vary significantly between different regions of Scotland.

10. Cultural Considerations:
While weather-appropriate gear is crucial, also consider the cultural norms and dress codes of the places you'll be visiting. Scotland's cities offer a mix of casual and slightly formal attire, so having a balance in your wardrobe is essential.

Dressing appropriately for Scotland's diverse and ever-changing weather is key to enjoying a comfortable and memorable trip. By packing a mix of clothing layers, waterproof outerwear, sturdy footwear, and weather-resistant accessories, you'll be prepared to embrace Scotland's stunning landscapes and vibrant culture, no matter what the weather brings.

11.2 Travel Accessories and Gadgets

Embarking on a journey to Scotland is an exciting adventure filled with stunning landscapes, historic sites, and unique cultural experiences. To make the most of your trip and ensure you're well-prepared for the various activities and challenges that may arise, having the right travel accessories and gadgets can greatly enhance your overall experience. From staying connected to capturing breathtaking moments, here's a comprehensive guide to essential travel companions for your Scottish escapade.

1. Universal Power Adapter:

Scotland uses a Type G power outlet, so a universal power adapter is essential to keep your devices charged. Look for one with multiple USB ports to charge multiple gadgets simultaneously.

2. Portable Charger:

Exploring the scenic landscapes of Scotland can drain your device batteries quickly. A portable charger can be a lifesaver, allowing you to recharge your smartphone, camera, or other gadgets on the go.

3. Travel-Friendly Camera:

Scotland's landscapes are a photographer's dream. A compact, high-quality camera or smartphone with a good camera can help you capture the beauty of the Highlands, historic castles, and vibrant cities.

4. Waterproof Phone Case:

Given Scotland's unpredictable weather, a waterproof phone case can protect your device from rain or accidental splashes while still allowing you to capture stunning shots.

5. Noise-Canceling Headphones:
Whether you're on a long flight or a scenic train journey through the Highlands, noise-canceling headphones can provide an immersive audio experience, making your travel more comfortable and enjoyable.

6. Navigation Tools:
A GPS device or a navigation app can help you navigate Scotland's winding roads and remote areas with ease. Offline maps can be a savior in areas with limited connectivity.

7. E-Reader or Tablet:
For avid readers, an e-reader or tablet loaded with books, magazines, and travel guides can keep you entertained during downtime or long journeys.

8. Portable Wi-Fi Hotspot:
If you need to stay connected, consider renting or buying a portable Wi-Fi hotspot. This ensures you have reliable internet access throughout your trip, which can be helpful for navigation, communication, and sharing your experiences online.

9. Language Translation Apps:

While English is widely spoken in Scotland, having a language translation app can come in handy for understanding local accents or communicating with locals in more remote areas.

10. Travel Wallet or Organizer:
Keep your travel documents, passport, tickets, and currency organized and secure with a dedicated travel wallet or organizer. RFID-blocking versions can also protect your personal information from electronic theft.

11. Multi-Tool or Swiss Army Knife:
A compact multi-tool can be incredibly useful for minor repairs, opening bottles, or cutting through packaging. Just make sure to pack it in your checked luggage when flying.

12. Reusable Water Bottle:
Stay hydrated while exploring by carrying a reusable water bottle. Scotland's natural water sources are often safe to drink from, so you can refill it throughout your journey.

13. First Aid Kit:
Pack a basic first aid kit with essentials like band-aids, pain relievers, antiseptic wipes, and any necessary prescription medications.

14. Weather-Resistant Backpack:
A sturdy, weather-resistant backpack is essential for carrying your gadgets, travel essentials, and extra layers of clothing as you explore Scotland's diverse landscapes.

Embarking on a trip to Scotland with the right travel accessories and gadgets can significantly enhance your travel experience. From capturing picturesque moments to staying connected and organized, these essential companions will ensure you're well-prepared to explore Scotland's breathtaking beauty, historical sites, and vibrant culture while making lasting memories along the way.

11.3 Travel Documents and Copies

When planning a trip to Scotland, one of the most crucial aspects to consider is ensuring you have all the necessary travel documents and copies. These documents are not only required for entry into the country but also play a vital role in ensuring your safety, security, and access to essential services during your stay. In this comprehensive travel guide, we'll explore the various travel documents you'll need and the importance of keeping copies while traveling in Scotland.

1. Passport and Visa:

If you're a non-UK citizen, a valid passport is essential for entry into Scotland. Ensure that your passport has at least six months' validity from your planned date of departure. Depending on your nationality, you might also require a visa to enter the country. Check the official website of the UK government or your nearest embassy to determine if you need a visa and the application process.

2. Identification:

Even if you're from a visa-exempt country, carrying a form of identification, such as a driver's license or national ID card, is advisable. It can be useful for various situations like age verification, renting vehicles, and making certain transactions.

3. Travel Insurance:

Travel insurance is often overlooked but is incredibly important. It can cover medical emergencies, trip cancellations, lost baggage, and more. Always carry a copy of your insurance policy and emergency contact details.

4. Accommodation Details:

Having a copy of your accommodation details, including addresses, reservation confirmations, and contact numbers, is crucial. This information will help you find your way, especially if you're arriving late or in an unfamiliar area.

5. Itinerary and Contact Information:
Share your travel itinerary and contact information with a trusted friend or family member. In case of any unforeseen circumstances, they'll know where you are and how to reach you.

6. Health Documents:
If you're carrying prescription medication, ensure you have a copy of the prescription and a letter from your doctor explaining the need for the medication. It's also wise to research Scotland's health requirements and be prepared for any health-related eventualities.

7. Emergency Numbers:
Keep a list of emergency numbers handy, including local emergency services, your country's embassy or consulate, and important contacts back home.

Importance of Copies:

Making copies of your essential travel documents might seem redundant in the age of digitalization, but it's a practice that can save you a lot of trouble:

1. Security:
In the unfortunate event that your original documents are lost or stolen, having copies can expedite the process of obtaining replacements or dealing with local authorities.

2. Accessibility:
While you might have digital copies of documents on your phone, you can't always rely on technology. Having physical copies ensures you have access to critical information even if your devices fail.

3. Smooth Communication:
When faced with a language barrier or unfamiliar procedures, presenting a local authority with a physical copy of a document can aid in communication and understanding.

4. Proof of Identity:
A copy of your passport and identification can be used as proof of identity when required, allowing you to keep your original documents secure.

Preparing your travel documents and copies meticulously is an essential part of planning your trip to Scotland. These documents not only enable your entry into the country but also contribute to a safe and enjoyable travel experience. Remember to double-check all requirements before you depart and to keep both digital and physical copies of important documents for a worry-free journey.

CHAPTER 12. Transportation in Scotland

12.1 Getting Around Cities: Public Transport Options

When exploring the vibrant cities of Scotland, navigating public transportation can be an efficient and cost-effective way to move around. Scotland boasts a well-connected public transport system that includes trains, buses, trams, and ferries, making it relatively easy for travelers to traverse cities like Edinburgh, Glasgow, Aberdeen, and Inverness. Here's an extensive guide to help you make the most of Scotland's public transport options:

Trains:
Scotland's train network is extensive and connects major cities and towns across the country. The main operator, ScotRail, offers services with varying levels of comfort and speed. Trains are often punctual and provide scenic views of the countryside. The Caledonian Sleeper is a unique option, allowing travelers to cover long distances between cities overnight, combining travel with accommodation.

Buses:

City buses are an integral part of the public transport system. Services are frequent and cover both central areas and suburbs. In cities like Edinburgh and Glasgow, you can rely on Lothian Buses and First Glasgow, respectively. One of the benefits of buses is their extensive network, reaching places that might not be accessible by other means.

Trams:
Edinburgh is known for its modern tram system, offering a convenient way to explore the city. Trams run through the city center and connect various neighborhoods. They are particularly useful for getting around areas that are well-connected by tram lines, such as the journey from the city center to the Murrayfield Stadium.

Ferries:
Given Scotland's geographical makeup, ferries play a crucial role in connecting the mainland to islands like the Shetlands, Orkneys, and the Isle of Skye. CalMac Ferries operates most of these services, providing travelers with a unique opportunity to experience Scotland's stunning coastal landscapes.

Smart Cards and Tickets:

Most cities offer smart card systems that provide convenience and cost savings for frequent travelers. The **Saltire Card** in Edinburgh and the **SPT Smartcard** in Glasgow are examples of these. They allow you to preload credit, making it easy to use various modes of transportation without needing to purchase individual tickets.

Day and Tourist Passes:
For travelers planning to explore extensively, consider purchasing day or tourist passes. These often provide unlimited travel on buses, trams, and trains within a specified zone or city. The **Edinburgh Travel Pass** and the **Glasgow Subway Discovery Ticket** are great options for getting around efficiently.

Tips for Using Public Transport:
- Timetables: Check the timetables for buses and trains in advance to plan your journey effectively.
- Tickets: Ensure you have the correct ticket before boarding, or consider using a contactless payment method.
- Mobile Apps: Download official public transport apps for real-time updates, route planning, and ticket purchase.

- Off-Peak Travel: If possible, travel during off-peak hours to avoid crowds and potentially get cheaper fares.
- Accessibility: Public transport in Scotland is generally accessible for individuals with reduced mobility. Buses and trams often have designated spaces for wheelchairs and strollers.

Exploring Scotland's cities through its public transport system is not only environmentally friendly but also offers a chance to interact with locals and experience the country's unique urban culture. Whether you're wandering through historic streets, enjoying modern architecture, or soaking in breathtaking landscapes, Scotland's public transport options provide a convenient and enriching way to get around.

12.2 Renting Cars and Driving Tips

Scotland is a captivating destination known for its stunning landscapes, historic sites, and charming cities. Renting a car can be an excellent way to explore the country at your own pace. Here's an extensive guide to renting cars and driving tips in Scotland:

Renting Cars in Scotland:

1. Driving License: To rent a car in Scotland, you'll need a valid driving license. International visitors may need an International Driving Permit (IDP), so it's essential to check the requirements before you travel.

2. Booking in Advance: It's advisable to book your rental car in advance, especially during peak tourist seasons. Online platforms and rental agencies at airports are common options.

3. Age Restrictions: Most rental companies require drivers to be at least 21 years old, and some may have additional fees for drivers under 25.

4. Insurance: Basic insurance is usually included in the rental cost, but it's recommended to consider additional coverage, like Collision Damage Waiver (CDW) and theft protection. Travel insurance with rental car coverage is another option.

5. Car Types: You can choose from a range of vehicles, including compact cars, SUVs, and luxury models. Keep in mind that Scotland has narrow roads in some areas, so consider the size of the vehicle.

Driving Tips:

1. Left-Side Driving: In Scotland, like the rest of the UK, you drive on the left side of the road. The driver's seat is on the right side of the car.

2. Road Signs and Speed Limits: Familiarize yourself with Scottish road signs and speed limits. Speed limits are usually 30 mph (48 km/h) in urban areas, 60 mph (96 km/h) on single-carriageway roads, and 70 mph (112 km/h) on dual-carriageways and motorways.

3. Roundabouts: Roundabouts are common in Scotland. Vehicles already on the roundabout have the right of way. Pay attention to road signs and lane markings.

4. Narrow Roads: Many rural roads in Scotland can be narrow, especially in the Highlands. Be prepared to yield to oncoming traffic in passing places.

5. Weather Conditions: Scotland's weather can be unpredictable. Rain and fog are common, so drive cautiously and use headlights when visibility is reduced.

6. Parking: Look for designated parking areas and pay attention to parking signs to avoid fines. Some cities have strict parking regulations.

7. Fuel: Petrol (gasoline) stations are widely available, but in rural areas, they might be less frequent. Plan your route accordingly and keep the tank filled.

8. Mobile Phones: Using a handheld mobile phone while driving is illegal in Scotland. Use a hands-free system if you need to make calls.

9. Seatbelts: Seatbelts are mandatory for all passengers, and children must use appropriate car seats.

10. Drink Driving: Scotland has strict drink-driving laws. The legal blood alcohol limit for drivers is lower than in many other countries.

Exploring Scotland:
1. Edinburgh: Visit the capital city with its historic castle, the Royal Mile, and vibrant festivals.

2. Scottish Highlands: Drive through stunning landscapes, visit Loch Ness, and explore picturesque villages.

3. Isle of Skye: Cross the Skye Bridge and experience breathtaking landscapes, rugged cliffs, and unique rock formations.

4. North Coast 500: Embark on this scenic route that takes you along the northern coastline, showcasing some of Scotland's most stunning views.

5. Whisky Distilleries: Scotland is famous for its whisky. Take a tour of distilleries and learn about the whisky-making process.

Remember, driving in Scotland can be a rewarding experience, allowing you to discover hidden gems and explore the country's diverse landscapes. Stay safe, follow the rules of the road, and enjoy your journey!

12.3 Train and Bus Travel

Train and bus travel are excellent ways to explore Scotland, offering convenience, stunning views, and the opportunity to immerse yourself in the country's diverse landscapes. Here's a guide to train and bus travel in Scotland:

Train Travel:

1. Rail Network: Scotland boasts an extensive and well-connected rail network, making it easy to travel between major cities, towns, and even some remote areas.

2. Types of Trains: The train services in Scotland range from local commuter trains to long-distance services. ScotRail operates most of the train services, and there are also some luxury options like the Caledonian Sleeper overnight train.

3. Major Routes: The Edinburgh-Glasgow route is one of the busiest, offering frequent services between these two iconic cities. The Highland Main Line takes you through stunning landscapes from Perth to Inverness.

4. Scenic Journeys: Scotland is famous for its scenic train routes. The West Highland Line to Mallaig offers breathtaking views of lochs and mountains, while the Borders Railway takes you through picturesque landscapes to the Scottish Borders.

5. Tickets and Passes: You can purchase individual tickets or consider rail passes like the BritRail Pass or the Spirit of Scotland Pass for unlimited travel within a certain period.

6. Booking: It's a good idea to book your train tickets in advance, especially during peak travel seasons, to secure your seat and potentially get better fares.

Bus Travel:
1. Bus Network: Buses are a reliable and affordable way to explore Scotland's cities and towns, as well as reach more remote areas where train services might be limited.

2. Types of Buses: There are various types of buses, including local city buses, regional buses, and long-distance coaches operated by companies like Stagecoach and National Express.

3. City Transport: In cities like Edinburgh, Glasgow, and Aberdeen, buses offer a comprehensive network that can take you to major attractions and neighborhoods.

4. Rural Routes: Buses are essential for exploring the Scottish countryside. They can take you to areas that might be less accessible by train.

5. Island Hopping: In areas like the Hebrides and Orkney Islands, buses and ferries work together to provide an integrated public transport system.

6. Tickets and Passes: Similar to trains, you can purchase single tickets or explore options like the Explorer Pass for unlimited travel within specific zones.

7. Booking: While some buses allow you to pay on board, it's advisable to have the correct change. For longer journeys or specific routes, you might want to book your tickets in advance.

Travel Tips:
1. Schedules: Train and bus schedules can change, so always double-check timings before your journey.

2. Views: Both train and bus travel offer stunning views of Scotland's landscapes, so have your camera ready!

3. Wi-Fi: Some long-distance buses and trains offer Wi-Fi, keeping you connected during your journey.

4. Travel Apps: Download travel apps or visit websites to stay updated on schedules, routes, and any disruptions.

5. Accessibility: Many buses and trains are equipped with facilities for passengers with reduced mobility. Check in advance if you have specific needs.

6. Environmentally Friendly: Train and bus travel are more environmentally friendly options compared to driving.

7. Scenic Stops: Some bus routes have planned scenic stops, allowing you to take in the views and snap some photos.

Exploring Scotland:
1. Isle of Skye: Buses and trains can take you to the starting points for hikes and tours on the Isle of Skye.

2. Loch Ness: Buses offer routes to Loch Ness, where you can explore the famous loch and visit Urquhart Castle.

3. Cairngorms National Park: Reach the heart of the Cairngorms by train or bus and experience the stunning wilderness.

4. Scottish Borders: Explore the charming villages and historical sites of the Scottish Borders using the bus network.

5. Whisky Distilleries: Buses and trains can take you to some of Scotland's most famous whisky distilleries.

Whether you choose trains or buses, Scotland's public transport system provides a fantastic way to experience the beauty, culture, and history of this remarkable country.

12.4 Ferries and Island Hopping

When it comes to experiencing the rugged beauty and untamed landscapes of Scotland, there's perhaps no better way to do so than by embarking on a ferry adventure and indulging in some classic island hopping. With its numerous islands, each offering its own unique charm, history, and natural wonders, Scotland's ferry system serves as a vital link connecting these remote locales to the mainland. Here's an extensive guide to help you plan an unforgettable ferry and island hopping escapade through the Scottish isles.

Choosing Your Islands:

Scotland boasts over 790 islands, each with its own distinct character and allure. From the world-famous Isle of Skye, known for its dramatic Cuillin mountains and Fairy Pools, to the lesser-known but equally captivating islands like Mull, Arran, and Orkney, your choice of destinations depends on your interests, whether it's history, wildlife, or stunning landscapes.

Planning Your Route:
Mapping out your ferry journey is essential for a smooth island hopping experience. Numerous ferry operators, such as CalMac Ferries and NorthLink Ferries, run services connecting various islands. The interconnectedness of these services often allows for flexible routes. Research ferry schedules, frequency, and availability in advance to ensure your itinerary aligns with your preferences.

Ferry Types:
Ferry vessels range from small passenger boats to larger car ferries. Some routes are quick, lasting only a matter of minutes, while others are more leisurely, giving you ample time to appreciate the surrounding vistas. Be sure to check the amenities available on board, especially for longer journeys, and consider booking tickets in advance, especially during peak tourist seasons.

Highlights of Island Hopping:
1. Isle of Skye: The crown jewel of Scotland's islands, Skye's ethereal landscapes include the otherworldly rock formations of the Old Man of Storr and the Quiraing. Don't miss the chance to visit Dunvegan Castle, home to the MacLeod clan.

2. Isle of Mull: Known for its diverse wildlife, Mull is a haven for birdwatchers and nature enthusiasts. Head to Tobermory, a picturesque harbor town with colorful buildings, and visit the Isle of Staffa to witness the unique basalt columns of Fingal's Cave.

3. Orkney Islands: Rich in Neolithic history, the Orkneys are home to ancient sites like Skara Brae and the Ring of Brodgar. The Italian Chapel, built by WWII prisoners of war, is also a poignant landmark.

4. Isle of Lewis and Harris: This island offers a blend of stunning beaches, rugged mountains, and historic sites. Explore the prehistoric Callanish Standing Stones and enjoy the breathtaking vistas of Luskentyre Beach.

Practical Tips:

- Weather Preparedness: Scotland's weather can be unpredictable, so pack layers, waterproof clothing, and sturdy footwear to adapt to changing conditions.
- Accommodation: Book accommodations well in advance, especially if you're traveling during the high season, to ensure availability.
- Cultural Etiquette: Respect local customs and traditions, and be mindful of the pristine natural environment you're exploring.

Embarking on a ferry and island hopping adventure in Scotland isn't just a vacation; it's a soul-stirring journey through time, culture, and nature's grandeur. So, plan wisely, pack your sense of adventure, and get ready to create memories that will last a lifetime amidst Scotland's enchanting islands.

CHAPTER 13. Language and Useful Phrases

13.1 Basic Scottish Gaelic Phrase

1. Hello/Hi:
   - "Halò" (HAH-loh) - Informal greeting similar to "Hello."
   - "Ciamar a tha sibh?" (KIM-ahr uh HAH shiv) - Formal way to ask "How are you?"

2. Goodbye:
   - "Mar sin leibh" (Mahr shin LEH-iv) - Formal farewell.
   - "Tìoraidh" (TEE-uh-ray) - Informal way to say goodbye.

3. Please/Thank You:
   - "Mas e do thoil e" (mahs eh duh hohl eh) - Please.
   - "Tapadh leibh" (TAH-pah leh-iv) - Formal thank you.
   - "Tapadh leat" (TAH-pah leht) - Informal thank you.

4. Excuse Me:
   - "Gabh mo leisgeul" (GAHV moe LESH-kel) - To politely get someone's attention.

5. Yes/No:

- "Tha" (HAH) - Yes.
- "Chan eil" (KHAHN el) - No.

6. I don't understand:
   - "Chan eil mi 'gad thuigsinn" (KHAHN el mee GAHT hoo-eek-shin) - To express that you don't understand.

7. How much is this?:
   - "Dè an cuid seo?" (JAY ahn kweet shoh?) - Asking about the price.

8. Where is...?:
   - "Càite bheil...?" (KAH-chuh vail...?) - Asking for a location.
   - For example, "Càite bheil am bàthroom?" (Where is the bathroom?)

9. My name is...:
   - "Is mise..." (Is MEE-shuh...) - Introducing yourself.
   - For example, "Is mise [Your Name]."

10. Can you help me?:
    - "An urrainn dhut cabhrachadh dhomh?" (Ahn OOR-uhn goo CHAV-ruh-chuh gohm?) - Asking for assistance.

11. I'm lost:
   - "Tha mi air chall" (HAH mee ehr khahl) - Saying you're lost.

12. I'm from...:
   - "Tha mi à [Your Country]" (HAH mee ah [Your Country]) - Sharing where you're from.

Remember, the pronunciation can be a bit challenging, but locals will appreciate your effort to use Gaelic phrases. Using these phrases can enhance your travel experience by connecting you with the culture and people of Scotland.

13.2 Commonly Used English Expressions

1. Aye - This means "yes." It's a common term used across Scotland.

2. Wee - It means "small" or "little." You might hear locals refer to things as "wee" quite often.

3. Braw - An expression that means "excellent" or "great."

4. Dreich - Describes the weather when it's gloomy, damp, and overcast. A word that captures the essence of Scottish weather.

5. Dinnae fash yersel' - Translates to "Don't worry" or "Don't stress." A reassuring phrase often used in conversation.

6. Away and bile yer heid! - This might sound a bit odd, but it's a playful way of telling someone to "go away and think" or "stop being silly."

7. Blether - To chat or have a casual conversation. If you're enjoying a friendly chat with a local, you're having a "blether."

8. Glaikit - Used to describe someone who's acting foolish or clueless.

9. Outwith - This word is used instead of "outside of" or "beyond."

10. Ken - Short for "know." If someone asks "Do you ken?" they're asking if you understand.

11. Hoachin' - If a place is "hoachin'" it means it's crowded or bustling with people.

12. Minging - Used to describe something that's unappealing or disgusting.

13. Scran - Food! If you're hungry, you're ready for some "scran."

14. Lang may yer lum reek - A traditional Scottish saying wishing someone a long and happy life.

15. Och aye the noo - A playful phrase that doesn't have a direct translation. It's often used to mimic a stereotypical Scottish accent and doesn't have a specific meaning.

16. Haud yer wheesht - It means "be quiet" or "shut up."

17. Square go - A confrontation or a fight.

18. Piece - A word for a sandwich or a snack. If someone asks if you want a "piece," they're offering you a sandwich.

19. Tattie scone - A type of potato flatbread that's a staple in Scottish breakfasts.

20. Bonnie - A term used to describe something as beautiful or attractive. You might hear people refer to the Scottish countryside as "bonnie."

Using these expressions will not only help you understand locals better but also make your interactions more enjoyable and authentic during your Scottish adventure.

Made in the USA
Thornton, CO
12/20/23 22:11:46

6311c052-de8f-415c-9a29-1397b5d56035R01